MESA VERDE
the living park

Text by Lawrence W. Cheek
Photography by George H. H. Huey

MESA VERDE MUSEUM ASSOCIATION

Mesa Verde Timeline

9500 B.C.	1500-1000 B.C.	A.D. 500	A.D. 550	A.D. 750	A.D. 1020-1130	A.D. 1130-1180	A.D. 1190-12..
First evidence of people in the American Southwest	Introduction of agriculture in the Southwest	Appearance of pottery in the Southwest	Basketmaker people settle in Mesa Verde	Beginning of Ancestral Pueblo culture (Living and storage rooms are built above ground; villages of fifty or more rooms appear)	Chaco Canyon "great houses" arise	Prolonged drought in Southwest; Chaco Canyon vacated; "great houses" built elsewhere	Cliff dwe.. built at M.. Verde an.. sites thro.. the South..

Text copyright © 2007 Mesa Verde Museum Association

All rights reserved. No part of this book may be reproduced, stored in a retrieval system, or transmitted in any form or by any means, electronic, mechanical, photocopying, recording, or otherwise, without written permission from the publisher.

Library of Congress Cataloging-in-Publication Data
Mesa Verde: The Living Park / text by Lawrence W. Cheek; Photography by George H. H. Huey
ISBN: 978-0-937062-27-2
LOC: 2007929641
Printed in China

0 9 8 7 6 5 4 3 2 1

Editor: Elizabeth A. Green
Design: Christina Watkins and Amanda Summers
Project Manager: Tracey L. Chavis
NPS Liaison: Tessy Shirakawa
All Photography © George H. H. Huey. Exceptions: Northern Arizona University p. 7 (eagle dancer), p. 25 (Hopi women), p. 47; National Park Service p. 29, 32 (both), 47, 51 (both), 52 (Wetherill), 54 (all); Linda Towle p. 61; San Juan Images p. 50; Colorado History Association p. 52, 53 (photographs); *Durango Herald* p. 53

Mesa Verde Museum Association
P.O. Box 38
Mesa Verde National Park, CO 81330
(970) 529-4445
www.mesaverde.org

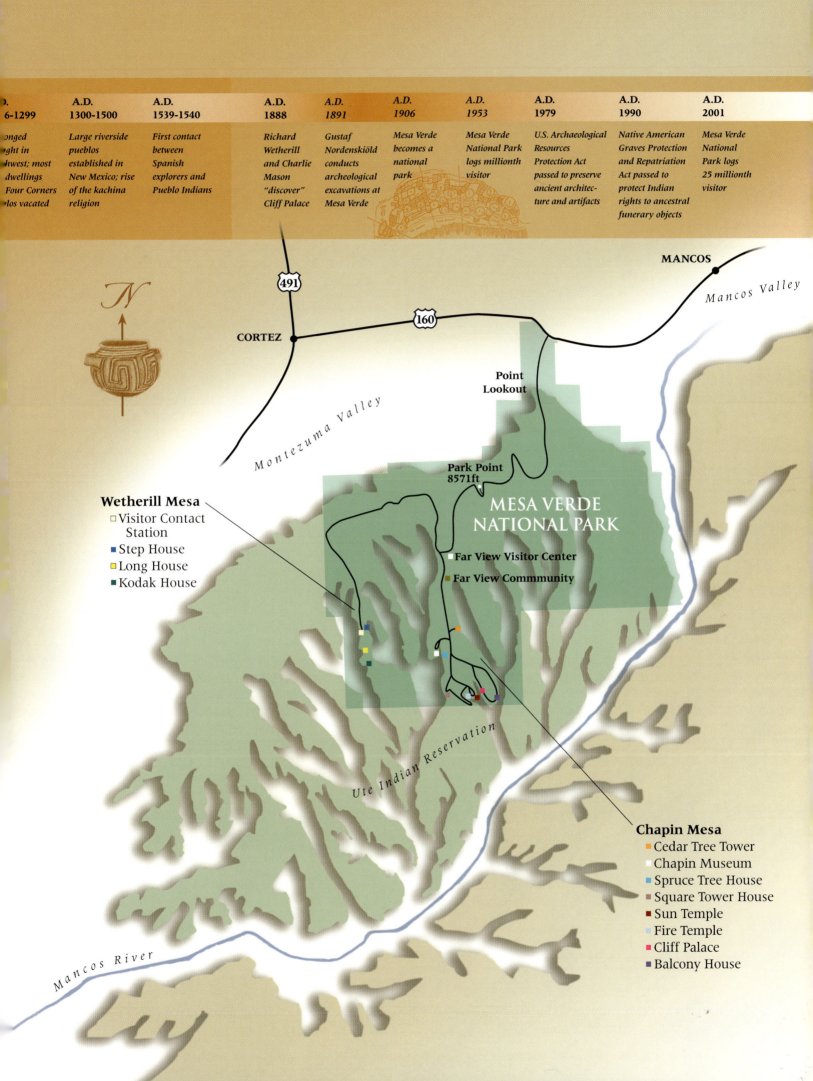

CONTENTS

1 THE LIVING PARK ... 7

2 PRELUDE TO THE PUEBLOS ... 9

3 THE ANCESTRAL PUEBLO WORLD ... 13

4 THE CLIFF DWELLINGS OF MESA VERDE ... 27

5 LEAVING MESA VERDE ... 33

6 MESA VERDE ARCHEOLOGY ... 41

7 NATURE, MAN & MESA VERDE ... 47

Far View House, part of the Far View Community.

THE LIVING PARK

On one warm August afternoon early in the 21st century, no one visiting Spruce Tree House Plaza was thinking archeology.

Earlier that day a troupe of Hopi high school students had traveled more than 200 miles to Mesa Verde to perform their traditional Eagle Dance at Chapin Amphitheater. After the scheduled event, the Hopis approached park officials with a request: could they dance in the Spruce Tree plaza?

Permission granted. Park rangers cleared the kiva of its usual swarm of visitors, and six of the dancers descended into it. After a long, pregnant silence, three emerged as eagle figures with great feathered wings and full head masks, and three others were dressed as hunters armed with bows and arrows. For half an hour the costumed figures stalked and danced as elder Hopis sang and drummed an accompaniment.

The park visitors clustered around were astonished and grateful to have stumbled onto an extraordinary event. For the Hopis, though, this wasn't about performance. The young dancers were carrying on a tribal ceremony anchored centuries deep in their culture. Maybe eight centuries deep, into Ancestral Puebloan times at Mesa Verde itself.

The surprise dance illustrated a vital point about Mesa Verde National Park. It is a living cultural park as well as a museum of antiquity. Twenty-four southwestern tribes today recognize the Mesa Verde region as a piece of their heritage. Archeologists continue to study here, and their discoveries keep inking in the sketch of life in the American Southwest before Europeans arrived—and the connections of that life to the present. Ecologists in the park are learning, and worrying, about human interaction with nature's rhythms. How, for example, can they manage Mesa Verde's forest fires, a natural cycle in southwestern woodlands, while protecting people and centuries of cultural resources?

Humans began investigating the natural resources of Mesa Verde and its canyons around A.D. 500. Here was abundant timber, natural shelter, water, and better farmland than the semiarid basins below could provide. In the A.D. 1200s came the great building boom of cliff dwellings, some 600 of them wedged into Mesa Verde's canyons alone, for reasons that still provoke debate. Then, only a few decades later, they moved away.

For six centuries Mesa Verde was left to the spirits. Then in 1888 a couple of Colorado cattlemen stumbled onto Cliff Palace, and it literally changed their lives—along with the course of archeology in North America. As more cliff dwellings were discovered, it became clear that such a cradle of cultural treasures cried for protection. On June 29, 1906, President Theodore Roosevelt signed the bill that preserved Mesa Verde as America's tenth national park.

As Mesa Verde is more than a museum, this book is more than a souvenir. It offers an introduction to the cultures of the Colorado Plateau that came before written history—the makeup of their societies, their hunting and farming, their art, and of course their most prominent legacy, the architecture of Mesa Verde. It reveals archeologists' latest thinking on the challenges these Ancestral Puebloans faced in a land of capricious climate and strained resources, and what forced them, in the end, to move away. And it tells the story of research at Mesa Verde, where southwestern archeology grew from infancy into sophisticated science.

Two vastly different cultures, over the centuries, came to treasure Mesa Verde. For different reasons, the place inspired each of them to remarkable accomplishments.

Kiva interior, Spruce Tree House

OPPOSITE—*Spruce Tree House plaza*

*Mesa Verde rises above the
Montezuma Valley.*

CHAPTER 2

PRELUDE TO THE PUEBLOS

Where did they come from?
For most of the 20th century, archeologists generally agreed on an answer to this fundamental question. Late in the icy Pleistocene epoch, glaciers locked up so much of the world's water that the oceans fell as much as 300 feet below today's sea level, exposing a land bridge across the Bering Strait from Siberia to Alaska. Some 11,500 years ago, stone-age hunter-gatherers—the first American colonists—ventured across this bridge and soon fanned across the mountains and plains of two continents.

But in the 1990s, new archeological digs in North and South America began to offer hints of possible human occupation thousands of years earlier. There are radiocarbon dates suggesting human presence in Pennsylvania 14,000 years ago and in Chile up to 30,000 years ago. New theories have proposed successive waves of migrants from different places in Asia, possibly using animal-skin boats as well as the Bering Strait Land Bridge. These ideas have kicked up storms of controversy, but they might help explain a thorny issue that has nagged archeology for more than a century: why did Native Americans speak some 900 different languages at

A light tan color represents what is thought to have been landmass 20,000 years ago, while the arrows indicate possible human migratory routes.

the time of European contact, many (such as modern Navajo and Hopi) totally unrelated? The debate rolls on, awaiting more evidence.

PALEO-INDIANS AND THE ARCHAIC CULTURES

In the Southwest, the earliest undisputed proof of human occupation remains the distinctively crafted stone projectile points and butchering tools of the Clovis culture, so called for their discovery near Clovis, N.M., in 1932. Beginning about 9500 B.C., Clovis people spread across much of North America, and in the Southwest they encountered a landscape that looked very different from what we see today. Where deserts now parch in the sun, there were cooler and wetter grasslands, forests, and even shallow lakes. Big game roamed the land—mammoth, bison, tapir, ground sloth, bear and fearsome cats half again as large as modern cougars. It was a hazardous environment, but Clovis people arrived with spears and atlatls (wooden handles that added leverage to a hunter's throwing arm), and they hunted in cooperative groups.

In fact, they hunted too well. In a pattern that has repeated itself almost everywhere our well-armed species has spread throughout the earth, extinctions of most of the large, plant-eating animals followed the arrival of people. The earliest Americans killed mammoth and bison skillfully and prodigiously, ambushing them at watering holes and driving them into natural traps, sometimes in herds. On the eastern Colorado plains around 6500 B.C., a band of hunters stampeded 157 bison over a cliff into a steep, dry gully, killing the huge animals with the fall. According to archeologists' reconstruction of the event, the hunters managed to butcher three-fourths of the kill, some 60,000 pounds of meat. Probably they preserved some by drying. But the fact that they didn't butcher it all suggests that the size of the kill overwhelmed the people available to use it.

Archeologists place the Clovis, Folsom and other ancient American hunters in what they call the Paleo-Indian cultures (9500-6000 B.C.). Next came the Archaic people (6000 B.C.-450 B.C.). Paleo-Indians were primarily meat-eaters; their Archaic descendants depended increasingly on gathering plants. They had no choice. As the sociobiologist Edward O. Wilson observed, "Humanity, when wiping out biodiversity, eats its way down the food chain."

None of these nomadic people left any architecture or pottery, so we know tantalizingly little about them beyond their hunting and dietary habits. We can identify different cultures only through the styles of their stone tools and projectile points. We do know that late in the Archaic period, probably around 1000 B.C., some Southwesterners began to grow corn and squash. The concept of cultivation, which had been practiced in central Mexico since at least 5000 B.C., slowly formed the foundation of civilization in the Southwest.

We tend to assume that the lives of the hunter-gatherers were short and hard, and that the dawn of agriculture and settled life bought them a new level of prosperity and security. But little in the ancient history of the Southwest is as simple as it seems, which is why archeology is always bristling with controversies. Agriculture, in fact, is a mixed blessing.

The large, beautifully worked projectile points of the Clovis culture bear witness to these highly effective hunters of the Paleo-Indian world.

As long as game is plentiful, hunter-gatherers spend less time than farmers making their living—finding and processing the food they need to survive. The wandering hunter's diet is richer in protein, more varied, and less dependent on the whims of weather. Once people make a commitment to agriculture, they have to develop more elaborate social structures and some form of government. Someone has to distribute the chores and coordinate the work—tending fields, maintaining irrigation systems, planting, harvesting, processing and storing food. Cooperation becomes essential. Meanwhile, drought, fire, and flood—the cyclic rampages of nature in the Southwest—become catalysts of famine and death. With so much labor invested in a settlement and its crops, people may decide to stay and tough out a dry year instead of moving on—and be rewarded for their perseverance by a whole decade of drought. As Emerson would observe more than a thousand years later, nature is no saint.

If their successes in hunting, gathering and reproducing had begun to overwhelm their environment, the Archaic people perhaps took up farming as a last resort. They began trying to manage their environment. In return, it also managed them.

THE BASKETMAKERS

One December day in 1893, a Colorado rancher named Richard Wetherill was digging into a southeastern Utah Ancestral Pueblo site sheltered in a small alcove. Two feet below the surface he uncovered the burial remains of several "cliff dwellers," as he called them. Three feet deeper, he unearthed a startling find: a different culture, apparently, that had crafted baskets rather than pottery, had hunted with the atlatl instead of the bow and arrow, and had rounder skulls than those he had found before in his Mesa Verde digs. He then took a leap of logic that would change American archeology. He reasoned that these distinct people had occupied the Colorado Plateau earlier than the cliff dwellers he had been investigating, because their remains lay deeper in the ground. His conclusion might seem obvious today, but Wetherill was the first to figure it out. He called his discovery the "basket people."

Wetherill was wrong about only one thing: he thought the "basket people" were unrelated to the pottery-making people who later built the cliffside pueblos of Mesa Verde. As later archeologists pieced together the Southwest's early history, they determined that the Archaic wanderers gradually settled down to become the Basketmakers (the term used today), who then evolved into the Pueblo societies. These transitions may not have been direct (or seamless). Some archeologists suspect these different cultural phases may have been triggered by droughts that caused people to move away, absorb new ideas from other places, then return. As the Archaic people settled down, they not only were working to improve their agriculture, but also to invent a new form of community life around it.

With their achievements eclipsed by the shadows of the

A simple pithouse was the early Basketmakers' housing solution for food storage and protection from the elements.

Puebloans' spectacular architecture, the Basketmakers (450 B.C.–A.D. 750) perhaps don't get the recognition they deserve.

Basketmakers are first known to have settled in Mesa Verde by A.D. 550. The first pioneers probably climbed the northern escarpment or followed one of the canyons up from the south in search of food or firewood. They would have found both in abundance. What they possibly didn't expect—it seems counterintuitive to us even today—was that they would find better conditions for agriculture on top of the mesa than in the river valleys and canyons 2,000 feet below. Cold air spills down the southwest-facing slopes of Mesa Verde and slides likes a wedge under the warmer and lighter canyon air, pushing it up and away. The growing season atop Mesa Verde actually stretches up to twenty days longer than on the canyon floors. More rain falls on the mesa tops than in the canyons, also making growing conditions more favorable.

Basketmaker architecture was far from spectacular, but it developed into a more-than-adequate response to the cold, sometimes windy winters of the Colorado Plateau. Early Basketmakers would scoop out a shallow, rounded pit and construct a dome of logs, sticks and mud over it. After A.D. 450 their pithouses grew larger, deeper and more elaborate, sinking as much as five feet into the earth and incorporating an entry chamber, firepit, storage pits and four load-bearing interior posts to support the roof. Modern engineering calculations show that they conserved heat much more efficiently than the aboveground pueblos that followed. They also were roomier. Many pithouses, however, were destroyed by fire. One theory is that they frequently caught fire accidentally, their twig-and-log ceilings being only six feet above an open hearth. Another is that most were ritually burned after they were abandoned.

Basketmaker "villages" were small, ranging from just two or three houses to about thirty-five. There was no apparent urban planning, but a few settlements featured a curiously large pit building that possibly served as a communal gathering place. Corn and squash came into their hands through seeds brought north from Mexico by traders. Beans later joined the menu. The people filled in their diet with native seeds, nuts and fruits, and game such as rabbit, deer, and turkey.

The Basketmaker culture was so named because of its finely-woven clothing and artifacts, such as this dog hair belt and yucca fiber storage bag.

They devised ingenious clothing and artifacts from the raw materials of their environment to make their lives more comfortable. Yucca leaves and fiber became sandals. Rabbit furs stitched together with yucca fiber became blankets. The Chapin Mesa Archaeological Museum displays an exquisite set of belts with decorative tassels and argyle patterns woven in the late A.D. 400s from dog hair. They also braided the indispensable yucca into bags and baskets in an astonishing variety of shapes and decorated them with dazzling geometric patterns. Baskets were used not only for food storage, but also for cooking. The Basketmakers learned how to roast or parch seeds in shallow baskets by adding hot coals to the seeds and shaking them together, and to boil water in pitch-sealed baskets by dropping in stones heated in a fire.

The agricultural life punished their bodies in ways that hunting and gathering hadn't. Basketmakers' skeletal joints reveal damage from endless hours hacking at the ground with stone hoes and grinding corn with a mano and metate. (The metate is a large stone with a depression, the mano a handheld grinding rock.) Stone grit from these tools would blend into the cornmeal and, in turn, grind people's teeth right down to the gums by the time they were in their late 30s. There weren't many who reached what we consider old age today; the few surviving into their 40s or 50s would have been considered village elders. Late in the Basketmaker era, people suffered a variety of health problems from relying too heavily on corn: osteoporosis, dental cavities, bladder stones, iron deficiency, and malnutrition.

But they weren't just struggling to survive. Villages grew larger and the Southwest's total population increased many times over. Modern archeologists can chart steady improvements in tools such as stone hoes. Basketmakers clearly treasured art and had the time for it after taking care of survival—one measure of an affluent society.

Three critical developments made life richer and easier for the Basketmakers. Between A.D. 200 and 700, people all over the Southwest gradually adopted the bow and arrow, originally an Asian invention. It was much more accurate and better suited to killing small game than the atlatl. Around A.D. 500 came pottery, an invention that filtered northward from Mexico. While the Basketmakers' method of boiling water with heated stones was ingenious, it consumed a lot of firewood and labor, and could not provide the sustained boiling that beans demand. Positioning a clay pot over a fire was much more efficient, and it made practical the cultivation of beans—a critically important source of protein.

With these advances in place, the people settled in the canyons, mesas and mountains of the Four Corners region were primed for the next great step.

Before turning more extensively to agriculture, the Basketmakers relied on gathering natural crops and hunting small game. Fletched arrows are evidence of their use of bow and arrow as weapon of choice.

CHAPTER 3

THE ANCESTRAL PUEBLO WORLD

The centuries from A.D. 750 to 1300 were fascinating times in the American Southwest. Population ballooned by 1,000 to 2,000 percent and a distinctive cultural mosaic began taking shape.

If an ancient cartographer could have drawn a map of the American Southwest around A.D. 750, it would have depicted three or more "nations" in different colors, but they would have had no capitals, no regional governments and only the haziest of borders. What was emerging around this time is what archeologists call "cultural differentiation." People of the Sonoran Desert of Arizona, the mountains of western New Mexico, and the Colorado Plateau were cultivating their land and building their settlements differently from each other, and not all the distinctions can be explained by their adaptations to different climates. They had become different cultures.

Those people of the Sonoran Desert are now called the Hohokam, a modern Pima Indian term meaning "all used up." In the valley where Phoenix sprawls today they built an incredible system of canals extending hundreds, perhaps thousands of miles, which literally inspired modern Phoenix's irrigation system. Hohokam neighbors to the south and east, ranging into the mountains of New Mexico and the Chihuahuan Desert of Mexico, were the Mogollon. The name, commonly pronounced "muggy-yone" today, refers to the mountains and plateau named for a Spanish colonial governor.

The popular term for the Colorado Plateau people, Anasazi, is burdened with cultural baggage. Early archeologists asked Navajos what they called those who built the prehistoric pueblos, and the Navajos identified them as *Anasazi*, which can mean "ancient enemies" or "enemies of the people" in the Navajo language. Many modern Puebloans consider the term offensive. Although the National Park Service and many archeologists have adopted the neutral "Ancestral Puebloans," the Navajo term persists in art and commercial markets.

This isn't by any means the complete cultural picture of the early Southwest, which by about A.D. 1000 had become bewilderingly complex and enigmatic—or so it seems to us today. In New Mexico a Mogollon branch called the Mimbres began painting their pottery with beautiful and bizarre creatures that may represent a distinctive religion and body of mythology. In Arizona, new cultures called the Sinagua ("without water") and Salado ("salty") arose, and archeologists still are not sure who they were or where they came from. In Utah, north of the Ancestral Puebloans, the Fremont people painted galleries of astounding human-shaped figures, warriors or shamans or perhaps spirits, on their canyon walls. The drawings resemble no other pictographs in the Southwest.

The archeological record of the Ancestral Puebloans reads as a cultural mosaic. Architecture and pottery designs differed substantially from place to place. So, probably, did ceremony and traditions. The Ancestral Puebloans likely spoke several different languages, which their most direct descendants, the modern Pueblo tribes of New Mexico and Arizona, have inherited.

One of the most intriguing developments of the Ancestral Puebloan world was the rise of a political and ceremonial center in Chaco Canyon, New Mexico, 90 miles southeast of Mesa Verde.

The unique topography of the Mesa Verde presented many advantages to early settlers.

Around A.D. 850, in a shallow desert canyon whose attraction as a heartland is impossible for modern visitors to discern, the Chaco people began to build a spectacular array of "great houses," creating architecturally designed complexes up to five stories high honeycombed with as many as 700 rooms. Unlike Mesa Verde, no forests embrace Chaco; archeologists have calculated that the builders had to cut down and hand-carry more than 200,000 ponderosa pine logs at least 25 miles for roof beams.

The Chacoans also built a network of arrow-straight roads, each twelve to thirty feet wide, radiating to outlying communities up to sixty miles away. Meanwhile, the canyon hub of these spokes amassed considerable wealth: archeologists have uncovered more than 60,000 pieces of turquoise shaped into beads, pendants, mosaics and inlays. Since the arid canyon had no native turquoise, and its great houses clearly were designed to impress, archeologists believe it was a ceremonial capital—and maybe a powerful political center, exercising control and extracting tribute across a sweeping arc of present-day New Mexico, Colorado and Arizona.

Despite the vast gaps in our understanding of all these cultures, we know this: the centuries from A.D. 750 to 1300 were fascinating times in the American Southwest. Population ballooned by 1,000 to 2,000 percent, a vast trade network arose from the coasts of Mexico to the mountains of Colorado, art and technology blossomed, and people clustered in increasingly urban villages. They learned to cope with drought, cultivate food more effectively, and create architecture that awes us today. In no other part of what we now call the United States is the archeological record so visibly rich as here in the Southwest.

EMERGING FROM THE PITHOUSE

Southwestern archeologists draw a line between Basketmaker and Pueblo society at A.D. 750, but it is an arbitrary divider. The culture evolved over several generations, not always smoothly. Late Basketmaker and early Pueblo villages existed on the Colorado Plateau at the same time. In a provocative theory, New Mexico anthropologist David E. Stuart suggests that the late Basketmakers were in denial, as we would put it today, clinging to an obsolete way of life even as their environment whispered warnings to change.

The word "Pueblo" is Spanish for "town," which in the modern world implies community planning. At the dawn of Pueblo society, scatterings of pithouses gave way to motel-like rows or arcs of above-ground rooms, usually arranged two deep: a front room for living, a smaller back room for storage. The Ancestral Puebloans of Mesa Verde hadn't yet learned masonry, so they built these dwellings with vertical wood posts held together with mud and clay—a type of construction called *jacal* (ha-cahl), another Spanish word. Joining rooms together as a block created a more stable

and durable architecture. It also might have been an expression of a more tightly woven, organized, interdependent community.

Pit structures still appeared in the early pueblos between 750 and 900. They were deeper and much larger than earlier pit structures, and probably were used for community gatherings or rituals. They were forerunners of the drum-shaped underground masonry structures called kivas. All these architectural changes suggest a society that was becoming more complex and more rooted in place.

More changes focused on producing and preserving food. Turkeys were domesticated to provide a new source of protein, helping to replace dwindling wild game. The Ancestral Puebloans invented or adopted backpack-like cradleboards, which "freed" women to grind corn while minding their infants. (Pressure against the boards permanently flattened the backs of the Puebloans' skulls, one of the anomalies that misled Wetherill into believing that these people were unrelated to the Basketmakers). The communities needed the women to be able to work while minding their children. Agriculture was becoming more intensive, with farmers trying cross-bred variants of corn in an effort to feed more mouths. Finally, there was a general migration into higher elevations as people

The first pueblos in Mesa Verde were constructed of jacal—vertical sticks bound with mud and clay. Attached rooms created a "block," with floors often a foot or so below ground level, suggesting an evolution from pithouses. Corn was processed using a metate and mano (above).

Hundreds of check dams have been found in Mesa Verde. Puebloans used natural runoff to build up soil, creating fertile terraces for the cultivation of corn and squash.

looked to the mountains and mesas for the rain that might yield better crops.

Conditions for agriculture in Mesa Verde may have been better than some lower lands, but they were still marginal in much of the arid Southwest. Corn is a finicky crop; it insists on a growing season of at least 120 frost-free days with a mean daily temperature no less than 55° F (13° C). A study of Mesa Verde weather records from 1978 to 1988 found that a theoretical corn crop planted on the mesa would have failed from freezing in three of those ten years, and a fourth year also would have been an agricultural disaster when only 1.65 inches of rain fell during the entire summer. The climate in Ancestral Puebloan times could have been better or worse in any given decade, but tree-ring records tell us that it has never been trustworthy. Farmers of every era have had to expect unpredictable and cruel extremes, and learn to cope.

The Puebloans developed several strategies for coping with the climate, starting with water management. Unlike the big desert basins of Arizona, where the Hohokam engineered irrigation networks several miles long, Pueblo lands offered only occasional opportunities for collecting and channeling water. Whenever the rains came, people made the most of the gift with reservoirs and stone check dams.

More than a century ago, archeologists realized that a round depression near Mesa Verde's Far View House had been a reservoir, originally nearly 12 feet deep and 90 feet in diameter. A system of ditches channeled water into it from higher ground. Besides the reservoirs, natural runoff on Chapin Mesa was reorganized by hundreds of check dams, small stone barriers stacked across drainages to slow the water and let silt build into sandy terraces that would retain moisture better than the mesa's natural soil. This was intensive agriculture, taking advantage of every possible plot of land that might support a cluster of cornstalks.

Long-term storage of food became an essential strategy to balance the unpredictability of wet and dry years. Nature has a vast arsenal of strategies to undermine human ingenuity, and Basketmaker food supplies had always been under assault by insects, rodents and spoilage. As the Puebloans improved their pottery and learned how to build solid, above-ground masonry storage rooms, preserving dried corn and beans for two or three years finally became possible—at least when there was a surplus to store.

Pottery appeared in the Mesa Verde region almost as soon as permanent habitation did, and eventually diverged into more than a dozen distinct styles—each of which changed only gradually over several centuries. Archeologists believe that preserving tradition and continuity in such a vitally important craft helped preserve community itself. And community—sharing the land, work, and food production—was in turn critical to the survival of all.

Southwesterners began decorating their pottery around A.D. 450. Painted designs were basic and tentative at first, then increasingly bold and elaborate. Earl Morris, a pioneer archeologist whose extraordinary ceramic collection now resides in the University of Colorado Museum, appraised the Ancestral Puebloan potters with deep respect:

In pottery making Pueblo art found its highest expression. The gracefulness of contour, and the dignified simplicity of ornamentation to be observed in some of the specimens, make one realize that the search for beauty was as keenly alive in the hearts of prehistoric Southwestern peoples as it is in our own today.

THE ART OF CLAY

Potters throughout the Pueblo world used the same basic techniques to produce their wares. They would begin with a flattened disk of wet clay, then build the vessel up with rope-like coils of clay, smoothing and thinning the walls with a scraper made from a gourd, stone or shard from a broken pot. Some vessels were not smoothed, but corrugated by pinching the wet clay coils with thumbnails as they were laid up. In cooking vessels these corrugations were practical, not ornamental; the potters were making smart use of physics. If a pot could offer more surface area to a fire, its contents would heat more quickly.

If the vessel was to be decorated, the potter would apply a thin layer of high-quality clay called a "slip" to provide a fine surface for painted figures. Pottery made in the Mesa Verde region usually wore a white or very pale gray slip decorated with black paint made from mineral or plant pigments. The rare black-on-red and red-on-orange pots excavated on Mesa Verde had been acquired by trade with other Pueblo people from what is now southeastern Utah.

Mesa Verde ceramic artists seldom painted animal or human figures, but they had a vast and fascinating repertoire of abstract geometric designs. There were bands of parallel rings, spirals, scrolls, interlocking curlicues, triangular mazes, elbows that folded in on themselves, stairstep-like ziggurats, lightning-like slashes, and checkerboards. Some of the same figures appear on rock walls as petroglyphs. Designers today see an obsession with symmetry and the tension of tight, parallel lines.

Was all this pure abstract art, or was each figure invested with some symbolic meaning? We can safely assume there was meaning, although we can't translate the language. Pottery became such a basic essential in every aspect of Pueblo life—think about the use of plastic in our time—that design must have conveyed messages, as it does to us. Decorated bowls were treasured so highly that their owners would sometimes try to repair cracked pieces by drilling small holes on opposite sides of the crack and closing the crack with yucca twine. Throughout the Pueblo world, the deceased were frequently buried with pottery, a presumed essential for the person's journey into the next life.

A distinct trend toward larger and larger villages emerged in the A.D. 1100s. This might have been an attempt to resist Chaco's power, or an echo of the Chacoan political system. Or it might have been an effort to reduce conflict over natural resources by organizing small, squabbling groups into large, cooperative ones. Whichever it was, it tells us that Puebloan society was evolving into something increasingly complex. Large communities need authorities and social hierarchies to make plans, organize labor, and resolve disputes.

Still, villages were typically built and vacated within the frame of one or two generations. It appears to modern anthropologists that the restlessness reflected the capricious climate, though modern Puebloans say that migration is inherent in their culture. Whichever it was, a few years of poor rainfall, early frosts, or soil exhaustion would present a stark choice: move or starve. This was no time of serenity and stability—the moody, frequently stingy southwestern climate has always guaranteed farming people a year-by-year struggle for survival, at least until the advent of modern irrigation. These Ancestral Puebloans were coping with a rapidly expanding population, trying new ways to address the spirits who orchestrated the rains, establishing trade and clan connections that would help them survive tough times, and, inevitably, working harder and more creatively.

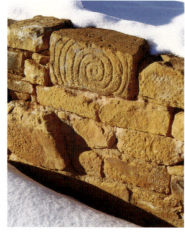

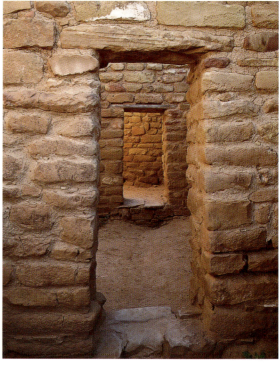

Far View Community was a complex group of pueblos bound together by family, cooperative farming, and the need for a central authority. Some archeologists think that Far View House may have been a distribution center for stored crops.

CLOCKWISE FROM TOP LEFT: *Pipe Shrine House; classic keyhole-shaped kiva, Coyote Village; globemallow graces kiva walls; winter snow defines kiva, Far View House; silent doorways, Far View House; incised stone, Pipe Shrine House.*

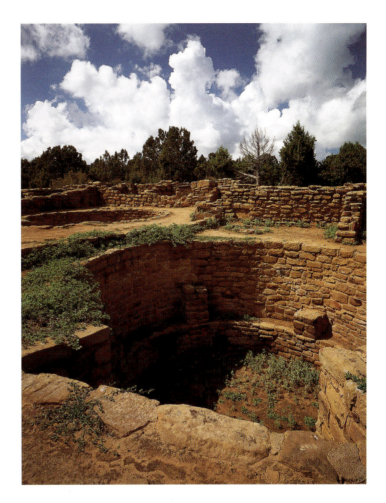

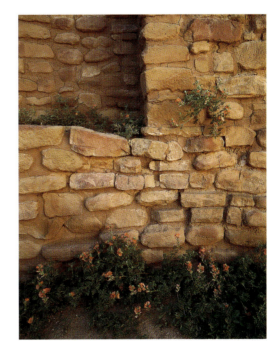

CHAPTER 4

THE CLIFF DWELLINGS OF MESA VERDE

Through most of the eleven or more millennia before Europeans arrived, North Americans' art, architecture and technology evolved very slowly—as we judge progress from the perspective of our frenzied age. Spear points changed relatively little across 10,000 years. Pithouses gradually evolved for more than 700 years before aboveground living came to be preferred. Little pueblos of 50-odd rooms first appeared in the Mesa Verde region in the late A.D. 700s; "urbanization" alternately surged and ebbed with favorable or discouraging cycles of climate. By the 1100s, however, some settlements appeared decidedly urban, with hundreds of living and storage rooms arrayed around a multistory great house, and many kivas suggested a high level of ceremonial activity.

Then just before A.D. 1200 came the cliff dwellings, pueblos tucked into natural alcoves in escarpments and canyon walls all across the American Southwest. Although people had earlier built pithouses and some masonry structures in many of the alcoves, there was no apparent precedent or evolutionary ladder leading to this astonishing building boom. And then, despite all the effort invested in the alcove pueblos, they were inhabited for less than a century before the people dispersed, scattering to the Rio Grande Valley of New Mexico, the Hopi mesas of Arizona and southern destinations even more distant.

The cliff dwellings marked a dramatic shift not only in architecture and the way people lived, but also in the apparent speed of change in those communities. Despite more than a century of intense study, archeologists still cannot fully agree on why it all happened. Still, it is a fascinating story, and it may be one relevant to our lives in the modern Southwest.

Why build cities into the sides of cliffs? And why, especially at Mesa Verde, do they seem to form such elaborate and

"Every well-sheltered ledge of rock, every cave of sufficient depth has been taken advantage of..." observed Gustaf Nordenskiöld in 1893.

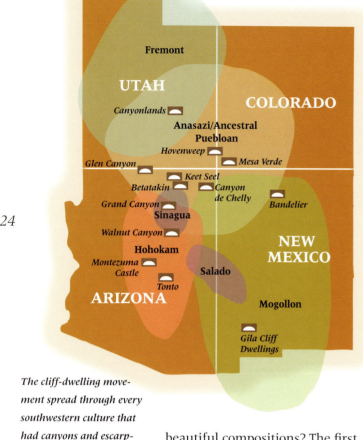

The cliff-dwelling movement spread through every southwestern culture that had canyons and escarpments they could occupy.

beautiful compositions? The first clue may come from a man who never saw a cliff dwelling, the 18th-century French Jesuit scholar Marc-Antoine Laugier, who laid out an ageless truth about civilizations and their architecture. Laugier wrote, "A building is neither more nor less magnificent than is appropriate to its purpose."

PUEBLOS IN THE CANYONS

In the mid-1100s, the vast pueblo "nation" centered at Chaco Canyon collapsed, possibly a casualty of a long, widespread drought that plagued the Southwest from A.D. 1130 to 1180. Some of the Chacoan people filtered into the northern San Juan Basin. They built Chaco-style great houses in dozens of locations surrounding Mesa Verde and Sleeping Ute Mountain. Escalante, built in A.D. 1129 near the present-day town of Dolores, Colorado, was clearly a Chacoan great house; it even echoes the distinctive banded Chaco masonry style. Rows of large stone blocks alternate with rows of small stones. Far View, atop Mesa Verde, may also have been a great house. The distinctive architecture could have been an effort to transplant the Chacoan political system into a new territory or it may simply have been people repeating the architectural forms they already knew—which is what refugees or colonists usually do.

But very shortly, around A.D. 1190, a new and even more dramatic form of architecture began to rise in the canyons of Mesa Verde. In substantial numbers, Ancestral Puebloans spilled down from the mesa tops and moved up from the desert basins, into the canyons and cliffs themselves. They occupied protective natural alcoves, sometimes near the canyon floors and sometimes several hundred feet above.

"Every well-sheltered ledge of rock, every cave of sufficient depth has been taken advantage of," observed Gustaf Nordenskiöld, the first scientist to excavate at Mesa Verde, in 1893. In these geologically accommodating canyons this meant more than 600 alcove sites, from one- and two-room structures that probably were storage buildings, to Cliff Palace, one of the largest known cliff dwellings in North America. There are many more cliff dwellings in the Ute Mountain Ute Tribal Park next door.

The cliff-dwelling movement spread through every southwestern culture that had canyons or escarpments they could occupy. Mogollon people constructed the Gila Cliff Dwellings in southwestern New Mexico, and the Sinagua made use of one of the few alcove sites in central Arizona in what we now call Montezuma Castle. In the Mesa Verde region there were not enough suitable alcoves to accommodate the entire population, which Colorado archeologist Richard Wilshusen has estimated at 12,000 to 14,000 people around A.D. 1200. As elsewhere, those who didn't move to the canyons clustered in large, densely packed pueblos, preferably atop mesas.

Early archeologists felt certain they knew why the cliff dwellings appeared. "Nothing short of the ever imminent attacks of a hostile people, can have driven the cliff-dwellers to these impregnable mountain fastnesses," wrote Nordenskiöld. Many modern archeologists have concurred. "There are some sites in the Grand Canyon located in unbelievably dangerous, difficult-to-access places," says Christian Downum, a Northern Arizona University archeologist. "There was no reason on earth people would have built there unless they were afraid for their lives every night when they went to sleep."

There may have been other practical reasons for cliffside living. As villages became larger, their dependence on agriculture intensified and food storage became an increasingly critical issue. Processing food—grinding and cooking corn—took more and more time, which meant that people needed reliable shelter for the daily work. In the plaza of an alcove-cradled pueblo it would always be dry and light. Dry pantry rooms, resistant to burrowing rodents, would aid the cause of preservation, especially when grain needed to be stored for a year or more. It is logical to separate work rooms, storage rooms and living rooms (just as we do in modern houses), and the natural shelters of alcoves offered protected enclosures for all these activities. Another possibility is that dwindling resources of trees contributed to the move into alcoves; natural shelters meant the homebuilders needed fewer logs.

Some canyons, unlike those in Mesa Verde, have broad, flat floors and flowing water. In Arizona's Canyon de Chelly, alcove living would have made more land available for cultivation and relieved the risk of flooded houses and granaries.

What about the aesthetic appeal of the alcove architecture? The distinguished American architectural historian Vincent Scully suggested that the dramatic cliff dwellings of Mesa Verde had symbolic meanings, perhaps illustrating new relationships (a mixture of tension and harmony, perhaps) between civilization and the natural world. Architecturally, these buildings appeared to be extensions of nature itself (anticipating by some eight centuries Frank Lloyd Wright's famous dictum that "No house should ever be *on* any hill or on anything. It should *be* of the hill, belonging to it ...") Scully acknowledged the obvious: we can never know whether or how the ancient inhabitants of the mesa viewed their sites as emotional or spiritual connections to the earth. But Scully wrote that to him, at least, "They appear much less like fortresses than symbols of dominion or instruments of prayer ..."

This much, at least, seems certain: No other Native American architecture, and very few buildings of modern times, engage in such a deep and powerful conversation with the land from which they rise.

But there were also disadvantages. In the 1970s, solar energy proponents adopted cliff dwellers

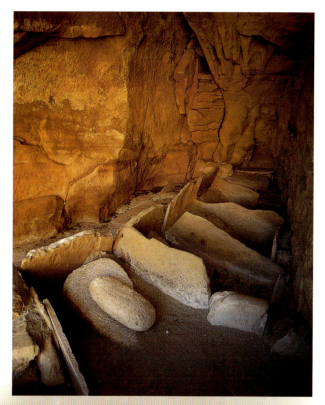

In the plazas of the alcove-cradled peublo it would always be light and dry— reliable shelter for the daily work and society of grinding corn.

as the founding fathers of enlightened energy conservation. Many of the pueblos face south, so they would appear to be passive collectors for the low-flying winter sun. Not so: Mesa Verde National Park archeologist Joel Brisbin, who works year-around in cliff dwellings, reports that the interiors are "bitterly cold in the winter, and only a roof and a hearth would make them bearable." It is true, however, that energy conservation would have been critically important to the Ancestral Puebloans, particularly when population grew and they gathered in large villages: once they harvested all the nearby firewood, the entire village would have no choice but to move.

Another disincentive for cliffside living is obvious to anyone who's ever climbed up or down to any of the less accessible aeries—Mesa Verde's Balcony House, for example. Nordenskiöld, a sturdy 22-year-old when he worked at Mesa Verde, complained about the climb to Spring House:

The many south-facing cliff dwellings of Mesa Verde suggest passive solar collectors, but appearances are deceptive. Archeologists report most rooms are "bitterly cold" in the winter.

"From the bottom of the cañon the buildings can be reached only by a difficult and dangerous climb from ledge to ledge; and a very circuitous route, either up or down the cañon, must be taken to scale the mesa ..." Imagine the Ancestral Puebloans carrying large animal carcasses, loads of firewood, or ollas full of water. Some alcoves have natural seeps that provide a ready-made water source, but they can dry up in droughts. Many cliff dwellings lie a long climb away from permanent streams and arable land. And some ascents would be even more hazardous in the snow, as they are today.

Toddlers growing up in cliffside pueblos would have to be watched closely. In fact, the entire community would be at eventual risk from the natural industry of geology, which continues to enlarge these alcoves by shedding slabs, big and small, from the ceiling. (In 1999 rangers at Navajo National Monument in Arizona quit taking visitors into the cliff dwelling of Betatakin because rocks were falling from the alcove ceiling.) And finally, there were the physical constraints. The alcove itself always dictated the maximum size and layout

of the pueblo, and restricted what its occupants could view from its vantage—an important issue if they were concerned about raiders approaching to steal or attack.

So were these defensive sites? And if so, who and what were the occupants defending against?

Nordenskiöld's 1893 vision of "a hostile people" ran into trouble as early 20th-century archeology became more methodical and intensive, and failed to turn up any evidence of the cliff dwellers' enemies. There simply weren't any archeological fingerprints of "foreign" invaders, no weapons, tools or personal artifacts, to be found anywhere around Ancestral Pueblo sites. Most evidence indicates the Athabaskans (Apaches and Navajos) and Utes did not migrate to the Four Corners area where they now live until the 1400s, long after the cliff dwelling period.

Moreover, the modern Pueblo people, the Hopis, Zunis and New Mexico Puebloans, had earnestly cultivated the image of being peace-loving people concerned most with protecting their cultural heritage from outside intrusion. This image, wrote David Roberts in his book *In Search of the Old Ones*, "projects backwards, half unconsciously, to create a kindred view" of the Ancestral Puebloans. In a modern world perpetually torn by war and ethnic strife, archeologists, historians and ordinary people all craved to find and celebrate an exemplary culture that actually had succeeded in a peaceful way of life.

In *Prehistoric Warfare in the American Southwest*, archeologist Steven A. LeBlanc summarized the defensive argument in what can best be called common-sense archeology:

Security must have been an overriding concern for the early inhabitants of the Southwest. Every individual, family group, and fundamental social unit would have constantly assessed their safety and security. Their lives, their family, their stored food and other valuables, and their land were potentially always at risk. Relationships with others—alliances—and the ability to defend themselves were the only means of security. There could be no appeal to a central authority, and a "tradition" of non-hostility could not be counted on in a time of food crisis or other catastrophes.

But other archeologists remain skeptical. Larry Nordby, who has conducted years of studies at Mesa Verde, finds the evidence for hostilities, particularly among the Mesa Verdeans, tenuous. For example, common sense would tell us that very vulnerable small sites of only a few rooms should exhibit more defensive architecture than the large ones such as Cliff Palace and Spruce Tree House, he says, but there is no correlation. The architecture of the cliff dwellings, Nordby believes, is about more efforts to ensure cooperation, rather than to cope with warfare. "It is likely," Nordby says, "that most residents knew about conflict occurring elsewhere and that knowledge may have shaped behaviors."

There is a middle ground. In some form, Nordenskiöld's "hostile people" likely were real, though their identities were constantly changing. They might have been wanderers displaced from a no-longer-productive canyon a hundred miles away, or maybe desperate neighbors. If there was "warfare,"

Many cliff dwellings have year-round springs that provided a modest but reliable water source.

it wasn't anything like the contemporary warfare of medieval Europe. The Native Americans didn't have the communications, the technology or the political structures to hurl massed armies at each other. (If the horse—the catalyst for so much progress and mayhem in Europe—had also been native to the Americas, the story could have been different.) Here, warfare probably was opportunistic—hit-and-run raiding, pillaging, and ambushing. Possibly nobody conceived of the organized siege, which would have been very effective against cliff-dwellers. When Coronado's troops besieged a New Mexico pueblo in 1540, the defenders seemed unprepared—they quickly ran out of water.

If some cliff dwellings were designed for defense, many of them are also beautiful and appear thoughtfully planned. Were they consciously designed to be beautiful, or at least to make impressive territorial statements?

We may never know for certain, but Laugier's principle is worth remembering. The cliff dwellings are magnificent for all the reasons we can imagine, environmental and social and political. They were a phenomenal effort of people being squeezed by circumstances beyond their control. Whether or not their builders considered them beautiful, building the cliff dwellings was an act of faith in their civilization in a time of great trouble. For that alone, they deserve our respect.

ARCHITECTURE OF THE ALCOVES

Like modern cities, the pueblos in the cliffs are composed of structures intended for many different uses: rooms for living, for storage and refuse, public plazas, kivas, and towers.

Most 13th century pueblos on the Colorado Plateau, Mesa Verde's included, are made of sandstone blocks, the material of the canyon walls and talus slopes themselves. It's a conveniently soft and brittle rock that can be pecked, chipped and abraded into brick-shaped slabs by using harder stones as hammers and chisels. The pueblo builders used ordinary mud and clay as their mortar, which they generally mined from canyon-wall benches near the alcoves or on the canyon floors. Sometimes they pressed pebbles and pottery fragments into the mortar, a technique called chinking, to improve a wall's stability.

Each mason built something of his personality or work ethic into his walls. With very little practice, it becomes easy to tell where one person's work ended and another's began. Some were meticulous and precise in their craftsmanship; some were decidedly casual—or perhaps worked in great haste.

The bare masonry we see today is not how Mesa Verde architecture appeared in the bustling 1200s. Most outside and many inside walls were plastered with mud and painted, usually with white, gray or pink pigments. Some hand impressions are still visible in the plaster, and their small size tells us that the usual plasterers were women or children. Certain doorways were outlined in a painted "aura," which may have signaled a resident's leadership status. In their day, the cliff dwellings featured color schemes that were as lively as their geometry.

The builders constructed their ceilings of juniper and pinyon pine beams, occasionally Douglas-fir, with layers of smaller sticks resting on them at right angles (the ceilings made of vigas and latillas in New Mexican "Pueblo Revival" architecture recall the Ancestral Pueblo design). The nest of sticks would be covered with juniper bark and mud, which would then serve for the floor of the room above. Doorways tended to be extremely small and

A glance upward in one of the towers of Cliff Palace reveals a hint of the lively, decorative plastered surfaces that once graced this pueblo.

MODERN MASONS OF MESA VERDE

An early 20th-century effort to stabilize one of Mesa Verde's buildings soars, with no attempt to conceal it, up an outside wall of Balcony House: a steel L-beam, bolted into the ancient sandstone. The National Park Service would love to remove it, but they aren't quite sure what the wall might then do. Today's stabilization crews work very differently: they take their cues from the ancient past.

The original mud mortar erodes ominously when exposed to water, so early crews tried replacing or reinforcing it with portland cement. But the sandstone was softer than the cement, so it would erode as water froze and thawed, then seeped through the walls, leaving only the cement. A better solution: replace mud with mud, at least when possible.

The Park Service actually uses a hierarchy of techniques today to preserve the architecture. In remote sites that are well protected from rain and closed to the public, plain mud is the perfect mortar. In walls exposed to water, the crews mix a compound of mud and an acrylic polymer. In walls that need to be fortified for visitor safety, the solution is a masonry cement bedding mortar. But all these mortars still are softer than the sandstone blocks they bind to.

Since 1957, the stabilization work crew has been predominantly Navajo men. Their vital role in the park dates back to the 1920s, when they constituted more than 90 percent of the maintenance labor force and lived in government-issue hogans on park grounds with their families. Their Yei-be-che dances became a tourist attraction at the rangers' nightly campfire talks. (The public dances ended in the 1970s when critics pointed out that Navajo dancing was inappropriate in the context of Pueblo culture.) Meanwhile, though, the Navajos had learned 13th century masonry on the job, which proved to be a useful job skill in the Southwest. Some of the workers have remained for as long as forty years, working not only at Mesa Verde but also on preservation projects at other southwestern parks and monuments.

A lot of the work at Mesa Verde involves backcountry projects in archeological sites so remote that a helicopter has to fly the crew to the nearest mesa top, and then they climb or rappel down to the job. The Navajos have a natural affinity for the landscape of cliffs and canyons; it's what their nearby homeland, *Dinetah*, is made of. Sometimes their beliefs complicate the work—they will not enter an archeological site if they sense that human remains are present. But their innate respect for the land also helps protect the park.

A workman stopping for lunch one day noticed a wire tied around a tree trunk. He took out his tools and snipped it. "It would have killed the tree" he said.

The Mesa Verde stabilization crew at work at Montezuma Castle National Monument.

inconvenient by modern standards, typically 32 to 34 inches high and with the sill placed more than a foot above the floor level. Mesa Verde men averaged five-feet-four-inches in height, women about five feet. Undoubtedly the openings were kept as small as possible to conserve heat inside. They could be "closed" with a fitted sandstone slab or woven mat.

One of the enduring perplexities of ancient Pueblo architecture is the T-shaped doorway, which occurs throughout the Southwest, from Mesa Verde to Montezuma Castle. Some archeologists suspect the T-shape had some symbolic meaning, or indicated a room with a ceremonial use. But at Mesa Verde, archeologist Larry Nordby has documented that in nearly every case, rectangular doors were sealed with a slab from outside, indicating storage rooms; while T-shapes were sealed with a mat from inside, meaning living rooms. The T-shape would helpfully admit more light.

Subterranean kivas evolved from the large community pithouse structures of the Basketmaker era. Small kivas were usually circular, but occasionally square or oblong with rounded

LEFT: *T-shaped doorways, which occur throughout the Southwest from Mesa Verde to Montezuma Castle, have puzzled archeologists for years. Most recently it is thought that they indicate entrances to living rooms as opposed to storage rooms.*

corners. Archeologists believe they served as gathering places for up to half a dozen related households. They may have been a part of the development of the clan system, which endures in Pueblo society today. Great kivas were beautifully crafted structures ranging from 34 to 63 feet in diameter and apparently used for large ceremonial gatherings. Social and religious rituals conducted in such familiar surroundings formed a social bond that kept Pueblo fabric from unraveling—just as the medieval church in Europe was doing around the same time with the unifying theme of gothic architecture. Kivas remain vitally important ceremonial centers in modern Pueblo communities, although their architectural form has changed.

Kivas in the Mesa Verde cliff dwellings were smaller than those of the Chacoan great houses because they had to be squeezed into tight confines. Most ranged from 11 to 16 feet in diameter with an appendage that gave the floor plan a keyhole shape. A masonry bench, or banquette, curved all the way around the inside wall. Roof beams rested on six sandstone pilasters raised from the bench. A stone firepit usually occupied the center of the floor, and a ventilator inlet in the wall supplied outside air for the fire. A clever (and essential) engineering feature was a low deflector wall between the ventilator inlet and the firepit, which would prevent an incoming draft from snuffing the flames or blowing smoke at the unlucky people on the opposite side of the fire. Smoke escaped through a hatch in the roof, which also served as the entry to the kiva. Mesa Verde kivas were well maintained; some have ten to twenty coats of plaster around the inside wall, with geometric decorations sometimes painted on each layer. Frequent plastering and painting were necessary to cover the built-up soot.

Many Mesa Verde kivas had a symbolic place of emergence, a hole in the floor between the firepit

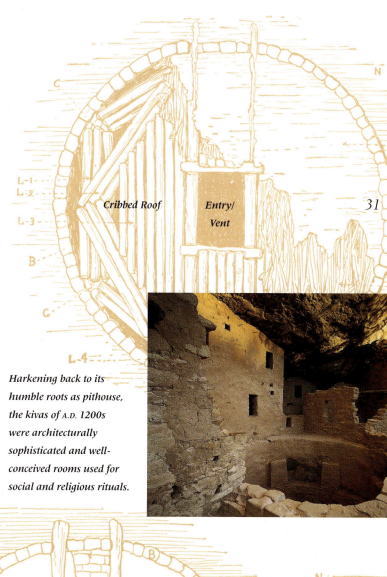

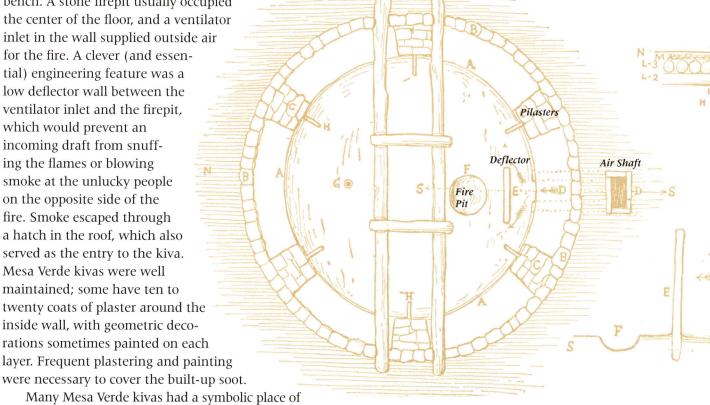

Harkening back to its humble roots as pithouse, the kivas of A.D. 1200s were architecturally sophisticated and well-conceived rooms used for social and religious rituals.

Like many towers in Puebloan architecture, Cedar Tree Tower has a tunnel to a subterranean chamber.

RIGHT: *In 1893, Gustaf Nordenskiöld published this photo of what he believed to be a look-out tower in Navajo Canyon.*

and wall. Pueblo history records that the ancestors emerged into this present world through the earth's navel, called the sipapu. The hole in the kiva was apparently a representation of this place. Some kivas also had tunnels connecting to a nearby tower, probably a ceremonial combination.

Small clan kivas, such as those in the cliff dwellings, may have served practical as well as ceremonial purposes. In his early excavations Nordenskiöld discovered a surprising variety of artifacts in them—fragments of hide, yucca fiber cords, cotton cloth, awls made of deer and turkey bones, pottery fragments, and stone tools. This strongly suggests that kivas were used as communal workshops.

They also may have been winter living quarters. Modern experiments have shown that a fire heats a kiva very rapidly, and thanks to the insulation of the earth around it, the room stays warm for a long time after the fire goes out. The large number of kivas and their smoke-blackened walls also argues for their use as living rooms. Although Cliff Palace appears to be a large village, only about 25 of its 150 rooms were apparently dwelling places. The remainder were storerooms. The number of kivas—21—corresponds fairly closely to the number of living units, and so many purely ceremonial kivas would hardly have been needed for so few families. Archeologist Stephen Lekson, in fact, isn't even sure these round rooms are "kivas," but rather may be the final and most elaborate evolution of that old Basketmaker dwelling, the pit house. And yet, the presence of sipapus argues that the kivas must have had a sacred dimension.

More than any other feature, the towers are what give the Mesa Verde pueblos their aesthetic verve. Forming city skylines in miniature, they punctuate the architectural compositions. Towers became common in Ancestral Pueblo settlements from A.D. 1150 to the late 1200s, and seem to have had several

Round and square towers punctuate the "cityscape" of Cliff Palace.

functions. Some free-standing towers had small wall openings precisely aligned so that shafts of sunlight would strike targets inside on the summer and winter solstices and spring and fall equinoxes. One remote round tower budding from the apex of a bell-shaped sandstone mound in Mesa Verde's Navajo Canyon could have been either a watchtower for signaling or an observatory.

Towers in the alcove pueblos might have had value as astronomical observatories in locations where the sun or moon would rise beside landmarks on the opposite canyon rim. They surely had ceremonial functions, since so many were linked to nearby kivas by tunnels. The square tower in Cliff Palace conceals an intriguing abstract painting on the southern interior wall that may have graphed the cycles of the moon, although this wasn't technically a tower in the A.D. 1200s—there were adjacent room blocks that crumbled later.

If the geometry of the towers had a symbolic reason—some were round, some rectangular—we probably will never know what it was. The forms never reappeared in the pueblos at Hopi, Zuni, or the Rio Grande Valley that followed Mesa Verde. But it isn't a stretch to imagine that their builders appreciated the punctuation of architectural grace and authority that they added to the pueblos.

Cliff Palace

No other settlement in North America, ancient or modern, evokes such an instinctive gasp of awe at first sight as does Cliff Palace. "This ruin well deserves its name," wrote Gustaf Nordenskiöld, "... for it resembles at a distance an enchanted castle." Frederick Chapin, the first writer to visit Mesa Verde, had a remarkably similar first impression: "There it was, occupying a great oval space under a grand cliff wonderful to behold, appearing like an immense ruined castle with dismantled towers."

Closer up, though, Cliff Palace more resembles a miniature city, a tightly packed urban experience—and an urbane one. No modern city's skyline exudes so much architectural commotion, and yet Cliff Palace's profusion of towers and plazas, kivas and condos, is infused with a swirling grace and rhythm. No modern American city appears to have been orchestrated so skillfully and also embraced its site so eloquently—and audaciously! Architectural historian Vincent Scully called it "a delirium of manmade geometry," a perfect description.

The earliest tree-ring date for Cliff Palace is 1190; the last log in it dates to 1279. Like most pueblos, it apparently grew with the community's population. Unlike the Chacoan great houses, it may not have had a detailed master plan; the shapes and placement of its structures were ordained by the alcove itself—although the builders did bring in several feet of fill to level the floor for their foundations.

Recent archeological studies have confirmed 150 separate rooms in Cliff Palace (an early survey estimated 217). Archeologists have determined the much smaller number of actual living rooms by the presence of hearths and smoke blackening. The peak population probably was about 100 to 150. A family living at Cliff Palace likely had a suite of rooms, which might have included a main living room, a storage room, a kiva and a shared courtyard. Although Stephen Lekson suspects that a single family might well have "owned" its

A large, fallen boulder was seamlessly incorporated into kiva and tower.

private kiva, other archeologists see kivas as shared rooms. Large public rooms, built at the very end of Cliff Palace's occupation, may have drawn crowds from other pueblos. Cliff Palace may have been, in effect, downtown Mesa Verde, its residents caretakers of a complex built for the larger community. The cluster of so many other cliff dwellings and Sun Temple close by supports this theory. We have no way of knowing what sort of gatherings took place there, but some possibilities are trade fairs, craft production, food distribution during hard times, or ceremonies intended to fuse relationships between clans, averting the prospect of war.

Cliff Palace may have been a special place to the Mesa Verdeans of the 1200s, who took advantage of a lucky break of geology—an unusually large alcove that could accommodate an unusually ambitious urban center. As an increasingly urban people since the blossoming of Chaco Canyon two centuries earlier, the Ancestral Puebloans would have gladly claimed such a site when they began moving into the protective embrace of the canyons.

Balcony House

Balcony House, built between the A.D. 1240s and 1280, is the most obviously defensive (and vertigo-inducing) village among the major alcove sites in the Mesa Verde canyons. "A handful of men, posted in this cliff-house, could repel the attacks of a numerous force," Nordenskiöld theorized. He also imagined that the dizzying plunge of 600 feet to the floor of Soda Canyon, or the spidery crawl to the mesa rim 90 feet above it, would not have troubled its occupants. "The perilous climbs that formed a part of their daily life, had inured them to difficult pathways," he wrote. "A few pegs in the walls, or a few projecting stones, were certainly enough" to serve as their ladders.

Park visitors today enter Balcony House by climbing a near-vertical 32-foot ladder at the north end, but the original occupants had no access here—they crawled through a narrow 12-foot tunnel at the south end. By any route, arriving or leaving had to be inconvenient. Balcony House enjoyed the luxury of a spring near the alcove, but it suffered a solar deficit because of its eastward orientation—it would never have warmed up on winter afternoons.

For modern visitors, the enigma of Balcony House is that its site implies a retreat of last resort, but the quality of its construction suggests just the opposite. The masonry is excellent, the blocks squared and laid with more evident care and precision than even Cliff Palace. The kivas are beautifully formed and unusually deep. The second-floor cantilevered "balcony" was probably most useful as a work space that enjoyed a little extra solar heat and light. It isn't unique to this complex, however. Other sites had balconies; this just happens to be Mesa Verde's best-preserved example. The three-foot-high parapet wall at the alcove's lip is unusual—but peer over it into the canyon yawning below, and its purpose is obvious.

Some openings in Balcony House are thought to have been used to view important solar events, while others were simply for ventilation.

Spruce Tree House

This third-largest of the Mesa Verde cliff dwellings was built between A.D. 1210 and 1278. Its site plan, split into two distinct parts by a row of rooms that served for storage and weaving but not living, suggests that two separate groups occupied the pueblo. Several of Mesa Verde's pueblos are separated into halves with restricted access between them, maybe signifying the roots of modern divisions between Winter People and Summer People in some Rio Grande pueblos. Each group is responsible for ceremonies throughout half the year.

Spruce Tree House includes eight kivas, a total of 130 rooms, and an intriguing open space at the back of the alcove. Nordenskiöld thought it was used as a pen for the Puebloans' domesticated turkeys, but modern Hopi elders have told archeologists it was a dance plaza. There is also a large, D-shaped "public room" connected, intriguingly, to a kiva.

The name "Spruce Tree House" refers to a towering Douglas-fir that once rose from the side of one of the kivas and towered above the rim. (In the 19th century, Douglas-firs were classified as spruces.) Nordenskiöld ordered it cut down so he could count the rings to determine its age. He may have thought it would give a clue to the age of the cliff dwelling. He didn't even come close; the tree was about 169 years old.

Long House

If defense was not a prime concern, Long House enjoyed one of the most benevolent locations on Mesa Verde—an unusually spacious alcove (about 130 feet deep by 300 feet wide) at the north end of a box canyon, facing south like a trowel-shaped solar scoop. The descent from the mesa is not difficult, and the talus slope below is not steep. Several seeps inside the alcove provided (almost) running water; we can still see the small channels and softball-sized collection chambers that the residents chipped into the sandstone floor. However, since Long House was the second largest cliff dwelling on the mesa with 150 rooms and 21 kivas, its residents still may have needed supplementary sources of water.

Nordenskiöld devised an elaborate theory regarding the defense of Long House. About 45 feet above the main village complex lie two long, narrow natural shelves, which the Ancestral Puebloans enclosed with masonry walls. Fifteen small openings, each just a few inches wide, were left in the walls. Although the ascent to the upper level was very difficult (again Nordenskiöld complained), and the interior space no more than three feet high, he suggested that archers could have been stationed there "to command all the approaches to the cliff-dwelling, and could discharge a formidable shower of arrows upon an advancing enemy." Modern archeological thinking is less dramatic: the small

openings simply were intended for ventilation.

Like Cliff Palace, Long House could have been a regional ceremonial center. It includes a large, rectangular, kiva-like structure, and archeologists suspect that the small, oblong pits in the plaza might have been "foot drums" with animal skins stretched tightly over them or wooden planks spanning them. With the alcove as a natural resonance chamber, they would have formed an impressive percussion section.

The unusually spacious alcove in which Long House was constructed allowed for 150 rooms and 21 kivas.

Square Tower House

Square Tower House, constructed between A.D. 1185 and 1279, is Mesa Verde's tallest building—it rises an astounding 86 feet above the alcove floor—and aesthetically its most assertive. The four-story room block claws up the sandstone cliff with fierce determination, even though the immense canyon unfolding around it can make all human-crafted construction seem small and fragile. Why did the Ancestral Puebloans build a high-rise here? It might have carried a symbolic message, or it could have been a technological stretch encouraged by the support of the unusually straight, vertical cliff. A free-standing tower would have toppled before reaching this height, and other alcoves did not provide such helpful walls. The complex once comprised eighty rooms; about sixty remain standing.

TALES OF THE RINGS

Today's most important tool for reconstructing an accurate picture of the Southwest's early civilizations was devised not by an archeologist, but by an astronomer.

Dates are critical information in archeology, because they establish the sequence of population movements, their growth or decline, and they chart the advance of art, architecture and technological progress. Before the 1920s, only instinct and educated guesswork could date prehistoric buildings in the Americas, and the guesses rested on no real foundation. Archeologists then had no baseline date for when people had first colonized these continents.

Early in the 20th century, a University of Arizona astronomer named Andrew E. Douglass began studying the growth patterns of pine tree rings in northern Arizona. He was trying to link sunspot patterns to climate trends on earth, which he did. But he soon realized that dendrochronology, as the science came to be called, was more immediately useful to archeology.

By 1929 Douglass had painstakingly assembled a complete sequence of southwestern tree-ring patterns dating back to A.D. 700. "With unbroken regularity," he wrote in *National Geographic*, "trees have jotted down a record at the close of each fading year—a memorandum as to how they passed the time." A year of drought would leave a slim ring; generous rain a wide one. By comparing a post, beam or half-charred log from a cooking fire with the master pattern, dendrochronologists could now deduce the exact year that the tree was cut down. (Unless the builders of Square Tower House recycled some old logs, always a possibility, we now know they started their work in A.D. 1185 and finished in 1279.) Scientists could also reconstruct the ancient climate year by year to see how it influenced people's migrations and social behavior.

Other dating methods followed dendrochronology. The measurement of radiocarbon decay, developed by University of Chicago chemist Willard Libby in 1949, can estimate the age of organic materials far older than tree-ring analysis allows—albeit with an error factor of a few hundred years. Pottery and tool styles also give away location and era of manufacture, which has proven useful in tracing trade routes and migration patterns. Dating petroglyphs and pictographs, unfortunately, remains elusive to science. It is sometimes possible to estimate the buildup of "desert varnish," or mineral stains, on the sandstone "canvas," but this is only useful in comparing the age of neighboring glyphs.

Like countless others who have peered into the Southwest's past, Douglass found himself totally engrossed, his life's course permanently changed. He founded the University of Arizona's now-famous Laboratory of Tree-Ring Research and acquired friendships among contemporary Puebloans, who would sometimes invite him to their ceremonial dances. "We have discovered a magic key to open mysterious books," he wrote in 1929, "and interpret the meaning of their writings."

Fire Temple

Fire Temple, near the head of Fewkes Canyon, looks like a ceremonial site. Like Long House, it incorporates what may have been a dance plaza and "foot drums" and a rectangular ceremonial structure with a band of white plaster across a wall, painted with images of rain clouds, cacti, people and animals. The architectural form and decoration anticipates the kivas that would appear in the Rio Grande area more than a century later. The site may not have been used for permanent habitation; only a few rooms surround the structure.

Sun Temple

This mesa-top complex is unique at Mesa Verde, suggesting that it was another ceremonial site. Fewkes, the first archeologist to excavate it, declared flatly, "This building was constructed for worship, and its size is such that we may practically call it a temple." Concentric double walls, filled with a rubble core, enclosed two structures that were either kivas or towers, and the floor plan of the complex echoed the "D" scheme of many Chacoan great houses built much earlier—although this is an uncertain connection. The shape also appears in ceremonial buildings at Hovenweep in Utah. Sun Temple's most perplexing question: why were its walls four feet thick, two courses of sandstone blocks with an inner core of rubble fill? The complex might not have been finished; perhaps it was intended to be a free-standing high-rise—a temple, indeed.

Many stories are told at Petroglyph Point in Spruce Tree Canyon.

CHAPTER 5

LEAVING MESA VERDE

One day in A.D. 1280, an Ancestral Puebloan cut down the final tree that would be used for construction at Mesa Verde. Archeology has not determined exactly how much later the last resident departed, but there is no evidence of anyone living on the mesa or its canyons after 1300. Just as people had left behind enormous investments of skill and labor in the great houses of Chaco Canyon a century earlier, so they left behind at Mesa Verde what we now consider the most beautiful prehistoric architecture in the American Southwest.

The emigration from Mesa Verde was part of a vast movement of people that encompassed the entire Colorado Plateau. Some kind of environmental or socially triggered cataclysm radiated even farther out. Long before the arrival of European explorers and missionaries, something dispersed, transformed, or shattered virtually every other culture in the American Southwest. The Sinagua began to move out of the Flagstaff area around 1220, assembled new settlements to the south and east by 1300, and then left completely by 1450. The Hohokam quit their vast urban complexes in the Phoenix and Tucson basins by 1450. And the great Mogollon city of Paquimé, the largest prehistoric pueblo in the entire desert Southwest (located in present-day Chihuahua, Mexico), slipped into decline after 1400, the citizens doing no more building except to subdivide ceremonial spaces into small dwellings. By 1500 even Paquimé was vacant.

For decades, popular writers, tour guides and some museums have heaped all this apparent tumult into a great pile labeled "mystery." Archeologists themselves often use the word, because the causes of the departure are complicated and controversial. No one agrees on a single explanation that wraps the great emigration into a neat package. But viewed from our own century of a rapidly growing, environmentally stressed Southwest, it may be not so much a mystery as a cautionary parable.

STORIES IN STONE

Discovering a petroglyph or pictograph is a unique thrill, a kind of communication across a vast span of centuries and cultural boundaries. We may not know what the symbol communicates, but it is still a tangible connection with people of ancient times—members of the family of humanity, like us.

Petroglyphs are symbols or pictures carved or pecked into stone. In the Mesa Verde region they usually were chipped into the dark patina on sandstone called "desert varnish," a natural film of manganese and iron oxide. Chipping through it exposes lighter-colored sandstone underneath, creating a negative image. Pictographs are painted with colors made by grinding natural materials such as hematite (red) and malachite (green) into powder and binding it with water or oils.

Certain symbols occur all over the Southwest; they may have been a *lingua franca* that people of all different cultures understood. Kokopelli, the humpbacked flute player, is the most familiar. He may be a spirit, a fertility figure, a trader, or a clan symbol. Many designs look like pure abstractions, such as spirals and mazes. Some are apparent pictures of events, such as hunting or dancing.

Mesa Verde's sandstone canyon walls provide many good "canvases" to peck or paint upon, but there are few surviving concentrations of petroglyphs in the park. The Battleship Rock panels were largely destroyed when layers of the rock peeled off following the 1996 Chapin Five fire. "Petroglyph Point" is the one panel accessible to visitors, reached by a pleasant three-mile loop hike south from Spruce Tree House. It includes human figures in several different poses, handprints, and animal figures. In 1942 four Hopi men visited Pictograph Point and interpreted a record of clan migrations. The square spiral represents the *sipapu*, where the Hopi emerged from the earth, and the scattering of symbols along a line depicts the wanderings of the Horned Toad, Parrot and other clans.

Intriguingly, some Southwestern figures appear on rocks all over the world: humans, animals, weapons and tools, topographic signs, and ideograms such as sets of wavy parallel lines. There are fewer differences in ancient petroglyphs and pictographs worldwide than in modern systems of writing. The basic human needs of water, food, fertility and a connection to a spiritual world were the same on every continent, and it would hardly be surprising if people expressed them with similar images.

When Andrew E. Douglass developed his tree-ring chronology of the ancient southwestern climate in 1929, a tidy explanation practically leaped out of his charts. A cluster of narrow rings revealed that the Colorado Plateau had suffered a widespread drought from A.D. 1276 to 1299, and those arid years corresponded exactly to the period that people quit building and left the pueblos throughout the plateau. At Mesa Verde, the final log was cut for Spruce Tree House in 1274; for Kodak House, 1278; for Long House and Cliff Palace, 1279. At Navajo National Monument near Kayenta, Arizona, Betatakin and Keet Seel both were finished in 1286. The last date for the Gila Cliff Dwellings of southwestern New Mexico was 1287. At Hovenweep National Monument, the great tower we call Hovenweep Castle was completed in 1277.

But a capricious climate had hammered these people before, all the way back to Archaic times, and it had never caused such sweeping dislocation and cultural change. These early Southwesterners were amazingly resilient; they had figured out how to survive hard times. They built up food surpluses and traded when necessary. They moved frequently to respond to changes in their environment. (Unlike Europeans of the time, they didn't seem to consider their villages permanent—the mean span of occupation for Colorado Plateau settlements in Ancestral Puebloan times was only eighty years.) Although the Great Drought was (and still is) a tempting explanation, it fails to tell the whole story.

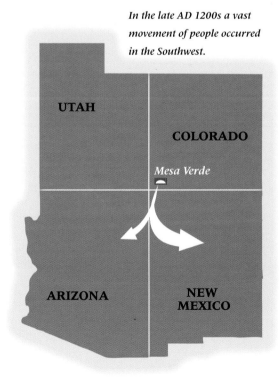

In the late AD 1200s a vast movement of people occurred in the Southwest.

Disease is an interesting candidate, because pueblos grew much larger starting around 1150, and tight quarters would have spread some diseases rapidly. But modern scientists have failed to find solid proof of any sweeping epidemic (although not all diseases can be detected by examining human remains centuries later). The bones tell us that (by our standards) 13th-century Puebloans had trouble getting enough to eat—protein, especially—but this had been a problem since Basketmaker times.

Another theory is called "systemic collapse." As trade networks became more complicated and critical to people's survival, any piece that dropped out of the network could threaten the stability of a whole region. A village that had a bad year and refused to trade or share its resources could send shortages reverberating through a vast area, like ripples in a pond. The more people there were to depend on these resources, the more delicate the system would be. A problem could lead not only to food shortages, but also to hostilities.

Some archeologists now believe warfare figured prominently in the great migrations. People began moving en masse to the canyon alcoves and remote mesa tops as early as 1190, but defensive measures accelerated in many places on the Colorado Plateau after 1250. More perimeter walls went up, ground-level doorways were bricked in, and access routes were blockaded. Some buildings were positioned for line-of-sight communication with other pueblos, presumably to signal trusted allies for warning or help. In one northeastern Arizona valley, the people of two hilltop pueblos went so far as to gouge a notch in a natural escarpment between them so they could signal each other. At Mesa Verde, the residents of Balcony House built new walls in the 1270s that suggest an increased concern for controlling access to and within the cliff dwelling.

Many skeletal remains on Colorado Plateau sites other than Mesa Verde record violent deaths. At nearby Sand Canyon and Castle Rock, two pueblos constructed in the 1200s, archeologists have found at least eleven victims of lethal skull fractures, apparently caused by blows from hafted axes or clubs.

"It appeared as though the inhabitants had left everything they possessed right where they had used it last," wrote Charlie Mason in 1888.

Climate cycles, disease, systemic collapse, warfare—all these theories don't contradict each other; they form a tightly woven fabric of events that makes excellent sense, particularly when we factor in the pressures of a rising population. These troubles were occurring in a land that had been stretched to the environmental breaking point by the accumulated generations of human pressure. Just as the Paleo-Indians had exterminated the big herbivores, their best source of food, the Ancestral Puebloans of the 1200s had reached the limits of many of the natural resources they depended on. They were cultivating every square foot of land that was feasible. The protein deficiency in their bones suggests that they had run short of small game. They had depleted the forests for construction and firewood—even on Mesa Verde. A ceiling in Cliff Palace built in 1255 employs straight, sturdy logs, but one built in 1278 uses small, twisted ones. (And if wood was a dwindling resource on Mesa Verde, imagine the plight of the Hohokam in central Arizona).

Extreme shortages of natural resources would cause trade networks and trusted alliances to collapse. Raiding, fighting and defensive fortifications would follow—tragically but logically, because people believed they had no choice. There was no Red Cross to provide relief and no United Nations to mediate disputes. "They could not declare themselves pacifists—to do so would have meant certain extermination," writes archeologist Steven LeBlanc. "In the past, war often does seem to have been about survival. Just because we live in an era of senseless wars does not mean war was always senseless."

Some Mesa Verdeans may have settled at Keet Seel 120 miles southwest.

By A.D. 1250, the Southwest was simply overpopulated. The strategy that had worked for several thousand years—pack up and move when you depleted the resources of your own neighborhood—was no longer an option, because all the still-usable sites had been claimed. When the great drought began in 1276, it was the straw that broke the culture's back.

WHERE DID THEY GO?

When the rains failed and the springs dried up, many of the Ancestral Puebloans of the canyons, mountains and mesas did the logical thing: they went to the rivers.

The oral histories of modern Pueblo tribes in New Mexico and Arizona suggest that their ancestors came from Mesa Verde and other Four Corners sites. Archeologists, taking their clues from architecture and pottery types, agree. Tree-ring dates from pueblos that arose in and near the Rio Grande Valley confirm a dramatic population boom in the 1300s, which meshes perfectly with the migration stories. But once again, the picture of the migration is a complicated one.

Not all the emigrants from the Mesa Verde region pushed southeast to the Rio Grande. At Keet Seel, a cliff dwelling in Arizona 120 miles southwest of Mesa Verde, a kiva built in the late 1200s bears the distinctive keyhole shape of the Mesa Verde kivas. Fifty miles south of Keet Seel, today's Hopi claim the Mesa Verdeans among their direct ancestors.

The people who founded the modern pueblos of New Mexico and Arizona came from several different cultures, because they speak different languages today. The northern New Mexico pueblos of Santa Ana, Zia, San Felipe, Santo Domingo, Cochiti, Ácoma, and Laguna speak Keresan. The others speak several different dialects of Tanoan. Zuni is related to none of the above.

Nor is Hopi, the pueblo with perhaps the closest links to the ways of the Ancestral Puebloans of Mesa Verde. The Hopis remain dry-land farmers; their principal villages still look out over the great red desert from mesas 600 feet high. Walpi, founded early in the 1400s and still occupied, has the air of an ancient pueblo. The Hopis joke that they claimed this land because no one else wanted it. They believe their ancestors include not only Mesa Verdeans, but also the Sinagua of Northern Arizona, the southern Mogollon, and even the Hohokam. The Hopis are the apparent broth of a long-simmered cultural stockpot.

In 1942, a Hopi Sun Chief named Don Talayesva described how the ingredients were added, drawing on his people's oral traditions:

Other peoples began to arrive. Whenever a new clan came, a member of the party would go to the Chief and ask permission to settle in the village. The Chief usually inquired whether they were able to produce rain. If they had any means of doing this, they would say, 'Yes, this and this we have, and when we assemble for this ceremony, or when we have this dance, it rains. With this we have been traveling and taking care of our children.' The chief would then admit them to the village.

Other pueblos may have accepted refugees in similar ways. If so, the question from our modern perspective is—why would they? World history teems with stories of ethnic strife, neighbors oppressing or killing each other because of differences in culture, language or religion.

Southwest archeologist Charles Adams laid out an increasingly accepted theory in his book *The Origin and Development of the Pueblo Katsina Cult*. The Katsinas (popularly spelled "kachinas") are Puebloan ancestor-spirits that serve as messengers between the human world and the gods, and the elaborate rituals involving them help to bring rain, fertility and health. The Katsina religion, or way of life, began to materialize in the A.D. 1300s, as documented on ceramics and kiva murals. And its powerful, pervasive rituals could have formed the bond that cemented people of diverse backgrounds together. Cooperation and the avoidance of conflict became a moral imperative, a critically important one after the vividly remembered strife of the 1200s.

And apparently it worked. The New Mexico pueblos of the early 1300s first formed on hilltops and took defensive postures, but by mid-century these puebloans were beginning to move down to the better farmland of the floodplains. Agriculture became more diverse (and therefore more successful). Hunting and gathering grew more organized and cooperative. When Spaniards first encountered Pueblo people in the 1500s, they frequently described them as peaceful and generous. (But as the Spaniards learned in the Pueblo Revolt, they were generous with their ferocity when threatened from outside—in 1680 they killed or drove every last Spanish priest, soldier and farmer out of New Mexico, not to return until 1692.)

Like all human endeavors, the apparent success of this great migration and reorganization was strewn with tragedies and failures along the way. Archeologists estimate the total population of the pueblo world may have shrunk by half to three-quarters. There are notable cases where integration failed. A clan of some fifty or sixty families from the arid Kayenta region of northeastern Arizona traveled 200 miles south to Point of Pines, an already occupied Mogollon village in the green forests near the White Mountains. The Kayentans built a "suburb" in their own distinctive architectural style, and produced their signature ceramics. Around 1300 the experiment went up in flames, literally. The Mogollons drove the Kayentans away and burned the entire neighborhood with all the belongings still inside the dwellings. No trace of the Kayentans ever reappeared there.

Nor did the Ancestral Puebloans ever return to the canyons and mesas of the northern Colorado Plateau, where they had built such astounding villages. The rains returned, and nature methodically rebuilt the depleted environment, but pueblo society took root and continued its evolution elsewhere.

And the new way proved more successful. After 1400 the arts and crafts flourished and quality surpassed anything the people had produced before the migration. Weaving, pottery and jewelry all grew more elaborate. Irrigation systems, at least in New Mexico, apparently improved crop production; people were living longer. There was still trouble ahead—the Coronado expedition would ride into New Mexico in 1540, bringing guns, horses and force-fed Christianity—but Pueblo society had survived by devising a new way of life.

The great migration was both catastrophe and renaissance. A culture that had endured so much hardship had to leave behind all it had built in one place and start over in another. This is the pattern of civilization. "In every great episode, or era, of creation, there are also unleashed hidden forces of destruction," wrote archeologist David E. Stuart in an insightful essay on lessons from the Pueblo past. "Indeed, humans as no other species live, create, destroy and die in elegant, repetitive testimony to the Doctrine of Unintended Consequences."

The question modern southwesterners might ponder, in light of many sources of information that the 13th-century Puebloans didn't have, is this: what are the environmental consequences of the civilization we have built in this beautiful, environmentally fragile land?

Walpi, one of the oldest, continuously-inhabited cities in North America, was settled in the A.D. 1400s; some Hopi trace their ancestry to Keet Seel and Mesa Verde.

*Jesse Walter Fewkes excavating
Far View House, 1916*

CHAPTER 6

MESA VERDE ARCHEOLOGY

The first modern American to take note of Mesa Verde was a geologist, John S. Newberry, who bushwhacked his way to the top of the forested rampart in 1859 and blandly reported: "To us, however, as well as to all the civilized world, it was a *terra incognita*." If Newberry had poked around enough to notice any of the mesa's man-made wonders, he might not have dismissed it so lightly.

Over the next three decades a trickle of pioneer prospectors found their way into the mesa, and they discovered a few of the cliff dwellings with troves of artifacts. One wrote, prophetically, that "a rich reward awaits the fortunate archaeologist" who thoroughly investigates the region. Archeology, however, did not yet exist as an established science. The people who explored and excavated the ancient dwellings of Mesa Verde would help to invent it.

Richard Wetherill was the key figure. A pioneer Colorado cattleman, eldest of five brothers, a Quaker whose pacifist convictions often led him to ride unarmed through hostile Ute territory, Wetherill's mind was a reservoir of intellectual curiosity that belied his dusty occupation. His formal schooling had ended in a Kansas high school, but not his education. Among other things, he picked up the Ute and Navajo languages, which proved useful on many fronts.

In 1882 the large Wetherill family homesteaded 160 acres of lovely Mancos Valley land, carpeted with tall grass and shaded by massive cottonwoods. As time allowed, the brothers began exploring the drainages of nearby Mesa Verde, and periodically they would stumble onto some of the smaller Ancestral Pueblo sites. On a portentous December day in 1888 Richard Wetherill and his brother-in-law Charlie Mason set out on horseback to explore Cliff Canyon, hoping to locate more of the dwellings. (There is a spine-tingling but maybe apocryphal story about the Ute elder Acowitz hinting to Wetherill of the existence of Cliff Palace, then warning him not to go there: "When you disturb the spirits of the dead, then you die, too.") When Wetherill and Mason got their first glimpse of the pueblo from the canyon rim, a miniature city of 150 rooms embraced in the rock, its plazas, towers, apartment blocks and kivas laid out in stunning geometric complexity, Mason gasped: "It looks just like a palace."

The two cattlemen spent several hours exploring Cliff Palace. Flushed with euphoria, they continued on to find Spruce Tree House the same day and Square Tower House the next morning. Then, riding back toward the ranch, they encountered three friends at a campsite, and the five men decided to return to Cliff Palace and collect as many relics as they could pack out. There were plenty to choose from. As Mason later recalled, "It appeared as though the inhabitants had left everything they possessed right where they had used it last."

This expedition transformed Wetherill's life. Instinctively, he understood that the story of these departed cliff-dwellers was far larger than he had imagined before. For one thing, Mesa Verde was a gold mine of antiquities for the Wetherills, and they were not reluctant to exploit it: they turned their Mancos Valley homestead into a dude ranch and escorted visitors on three-day cliff dwelling tours for five dollars a head. The tourists were invited to pack out whatever artifacts they could carry—incredible by today's standards, but perfectly legal at the time. The Wetherills also sold the pieces they excavated, which at the time was a legal and widespread practice. Richard, however, was nagged by the feeling that Mesa Verde's treasures deserved professional care. He wrote to the directors of both the Smithsonian Institution and Harvard's Peabody Museum, asking them to sponsor the Wetherills' excavations or join in the work at Mesa Verde. Both declined.

Meanwhile, however, a trickle of scientists found their way to the Wetherill ranch. Richard escorted them and worked alongside them in

Gustaf Nordenskiöld and his book "The Cliff Dwellers of the Mesa Verde" (upper left).

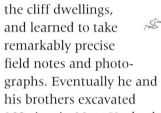

This 1890 newspaper illustration accompanied an article written by Frederick Chapin.

the cliff dwellings, and learned to take remarkably precise field notes and photographs. Eventually he and his brothers excavated 182 sites in Mesa Verde alone, plus dozens of others in Utah, New Mexico, and Arizona—more than any other amateur or professional archeologist who followed. While controversy and criticism have swirled for generations around their methods and commercialization, it is unlikely that any other amateurs in the 1890s would have proven to be superior custodians of Mesa Verde. It would be another generation before even professionals understood how a single displaced artifact could rip a permanent gash in the narrative. The Wetherills' work, wrote John Otis Brew, a later director of the Peabody, "can be argued as the most far-reaching single event in Southwestern archaeology."

Richard Wetherill

Eventually, Richard Wetherill's methods (along with academia's predictable prejudice against a presumptuous cowboy) got him banned from excavating on government property in 1902. Tragically and ironically, his life ended in 1910 at Chaco Canyon, where he spent his late years operating a trading post. In a tangled dispute over an allegedly stolen horse, a Navajo shot him to death.

Mesa Verde's endangerment came from its inevitable exposure, and it escalated quickly. In 1889 Frederick Chapin, a writer and mountaineer, happened onto the Wetherills' ranch and took a guided tour to the cliff dwellings. He found he enjoyed the challenges of "scaling cliffs" and employing the same rocky handholds that the Ancestral Puebloans had used for access 700 years before. His romantic 1892 book, *The Land of the Cliff-Dwellers*, alerted the world to Mesa Verde.

Nordenskiöld appeared after hearing rumors about the antiquities of Mesa Verde around the same time. He planned just a week's stay in 1891, but he got hooked, spent more than two months excavating and taking excellent documentary photos, and in 1893 published the first definitive book about Mesa Verde. *The Cliff Dwellers of the Mesa Verde* is still in print today, a model of clear-eyed archeology and insight, even if some of its conclusions are tinted by associations with the feudal Europe of his understanding. Ironically, Nordenskiöld was arrested when he tried to ship several crates of artifacts, including a mummy, back to Sweden. Coloradans were beginning to feel protective, or maybe just chauvinistic, about the antiquities nested in their canyons. In a letter Nordenskiöld sent home the day before the arrest, he complained that "an ignorant newspaper article containing expressions such as 'vandalism,' 'robbery,' and 'must be stopped at once' appeared soon after I had made my first shipment, which is why

I prefer to get the rest of my collection to safety as soon as possible." After a week of political maneuvering in Washington, the charges were dismissed, and Nordenskiöld was allowed to ship "his" collection overseas. (It remains in the National Museum of Finland.)

The newspaper article perhaps selected the wrong target. By the mid-1890s, Coloradans from nearby towns were staging Sunday pothunting picnics in the canyons. Relics were regularly carted off to Durango for sale. A few serious preservationists, appalled at the casual looting of the cliff dwellings, adopted Mesa Verde as their cause. Colorado Springs writer and poet Virginia McClurg launched a passionate campaign to have Mesa Verde incorporated and protected as a park. "The Cliff Palace is the prey of the spoiler, soon it will be too late ..." she warned, rightly. In 1900 she incorporated a nucleus of determined women as the Colorado Cliff Dwellings Association, modeled after a women's organization that had taken over preservation and management of George Washington's home, Mount Vernon. What form of protection Mesa Verde needed became a surprisingly divisive issue. McClurg trusted neither the state nor the "faceless bureaucracy" of the federal government. Other advocates furiously lobbied for a national park. Finally in 1906, President Theodore Roosevelt signed the bill creating Mesa Verde National Park. Although Arizona's Casa Grande, a Hohokam highrise from the 1300s, had been designated a national monument in 1889, Mesa Verde was the first archeological site in the world to gain the status of a national park.

For its first twenty-odd years, Mesa Verde National Park attracted relatively small crowds because of its remote location and poor roads. Many of the cliff dwellings looked more like rubble mounds than actual dwellings; they were a far less dramatic sight than the cleaned-up and

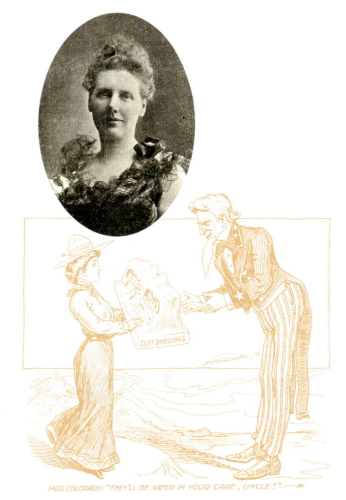

For 24 years Virginia McClurg campaigned passionately for protection of Colorado cliff dwellings. Mesa Verde National Park was created by Congress in 1906. Prior to coming under federal jurisdiction Coloradans from nearby towns regularly held pothunting picnics in the canyons of Mesa Verde.

Archeology at Mesa Verde has matured over the years and has become "non-invasive" and more reliant on ethnology.

CLOCKWISE FROM TOP RIGHT:
Jesse Nusbaum at Balcony House, 1910. Larry Nordby, Cliff Palace, 1996. Douglas Osborne, Wetherill Mesa Project, 1962.

stabilized sites visitors enjoy today. In 1928 a quarter of a million people visited Colorado's Rocky Mountain National Park; just 16,800 found Mesa Verde.

But the first professional archeologist to become superintendent of the park, Jesse Nusbaum, made dramatic improvements. He cancelled coal mining and cattle grazing leases on the mesa, and ended the practice of tourists scampering unsupervised through the cliff dwellings. He took notice of the shortage of employment opportunities on the nearby Navajo Reservation and made a point of hiring Navajos to work in the park. He built a six-bed infirmary for park staff and visitors. And he started the practice, now common in the national park service, of having rangers give guided tours and talks. (One tourist complained that a ranger used "too big words." Nusbaum investigated and supported his ranger, but he did advise the park service experts to stop using "unusual and obscure words.")

In the 1930s, Mesa Verde enjoyed the benefits of one of President Franklin D. Roosevelt's most successful depression-era programs, the Civilian Conservation Corps (CCC). Young CCC men signed on for six-month tours of duty at the park, earning $30 a month and performing a surprising array of work—helping archeologists excavate, reconstructing pots from shards, fighting fires, and, oddly, hunting porcupines with .22-caliber rifles. Park administrators thought the prickly creatures were damaging trees with their eating habits.

The science of archeology matured by trial and error at Mesa Verde, as it did all around the Southwest. For twenty years, beginning early in the 1900s, the well-known southwestern archeologist Jesse Walter Fewkes worked off and on at Mesa Verde, excavating and repairing various cliff dwellings and giving lectures to visitors (which evolved into the park's summer "campfire talks"). Although others later criticized his work (an occupational hazard in southwestern archeology now, as then), he built on the foundation solidly established by Nordenskiöld and Richard Wetherill.

The most intensive archeology in the park's history came with the Wetherill Mesa Project beginning in 1958. The U.S. government and the

National Geographic Society provided the funds. By the time the project was finished in 1965, hundreds of new sites had been studied and a whole new region of the park, with its spectacular pueblos of Long House and Step House, opened to the public.

Wetherill Mesa not only enhanced the range of experiences available to visitors; it also relieved some of the crowd pressures on the more famous pueblos of Cliff Palace, Spruce Tree House and Balcony House. By the 1960s, Mesa Verde's summer crowds had become a teeming problem. A 1965 superintendent's report claimed, in surprising frankness, that at Cliff Palace "bedlam is the rule of the day all summer long." With the rangers forced to "yell above the racket ... interpretation at this site is rapidly becoming a farce."

Today's summer crowds still teem at Mesa Verde, but it seems the visitor culture has changed. People are more respectful of antiquity; "bedlam" is rare.

Archeology today has become an intricate and precise science; we know more about the social organization, lifestyle, diet, art, architecture and migrations than pioneers such as Nordenskiöld and Fewkes could ever have dreamed. Still, more questions than answers swirl about the prehistoric Southwest, and any crowd of archeologists will churn with a tempest of opinions.

At Mesa Verde, the study techniques have changed. Instead of digging, scientists try to practice "non-invasive archeology," attempting to discern the social organization of a pueblo from its architecture. A loose-knit clan of amateur archeologists also have made good progress in enlightening some of Richard Wetherill's original work by practicing something they call "reverse archeology." Wetherill often failed to note where he dug up the artifacts that later made it into museum collections, but these sleuths have been able to match materials with their sites using Wetherill's photographs.

Archeology has also engaged ethnology, to its benefit. Archeologists work up their theories, and talk to members of modern Pueblo tribes, such as the Hopi and Zuni, to learn whether the modern interpretations mesh with Native American oral traditions. If they do, the conclusions are strengthened.

Archeology and Native American belief may never coincide perfectly, but each will always have something to teach the other.

RETURNING WHAT IS THEIRS

American Indians have long simmered over what they viewed as archeology's cavalier treatment and outright theft of their ancestors' remains. Congress finally responded in 1990 by passing the Native American Graves Protection and Repatriation Act (NAGPRA). The act radically transformed the techniques of American archeology, and changed the way that Mesa Verde and other national parks conduct research and exhibit artifacts.

NAGPRA requires that federally funded museums and laboratories inventory all their artifacts and human remains, determine which modern tribes might have ancestral links to them, and return human remains, items associated with burials, sacred objects, and articles of " cultural patrimony," meaning things that belonged to a tribe as a whole. While the law hasn't solved all the problems—it's often not clear what are sacred objects—it has at least provided a framework for negotiations.

Mesa Verde has had in its care one of the largest collections of human remains and grave goods of any national park. Twelve years of negotiations with all modern Pueblo tribes, two Ute Tribes and the Navajos—which all claim ancestral links to Mesa Verde—culminated in 2006 with the reinterment of those remains and objects. Tribal elders oversaw the private ceremony placing them in a final resting place in the park, thus allowing the spirits of their ancestors to continue on their journey.

Whenever park plans conflict with native beliefs or sensitivities, alternative solutions are discussed. For example, some tribal members felt placing luminarias inside some of the cliff dwellings for the holiday season was disrespectful. Now, the brown-bagged candles line the paths while lanterns light the dwellings. The park staff tries to involve the tribes in every facet of research and operation, respecting the tribal belief that Mesa Verde is their ancestral home.

CHAPTER 7
NATURE, MAN & MESA VERDE

The mountains of the American Southwest punctuate the landscape in an endless variety of shapes and colors, and their ridges and slopes and canyons harbor an astonishingly rich inventory of life. These are complex environments, where forks and turns in a corkscrewing canyon can create a mosaic of microclimates, and each environment offers opportunities for different species. A pinyon-juniper forest here, sagebrush and cheatgrass just around the next bend.

Mesa Verde (Spanish for "green table"), is neither a mountain nor a mesa, but a formation called a cuesta ("slope"), furrowed by a labyrinth of canyons. These provide habitat for more than 1,000 species of insects, nearly 600 different native plants, 200 birds, 74 mammals, 16 reptiles, 5 amphibians, and in the Mancos River curling around its base on the east and south, 5 native species of fish.

But for all of the mesa's fertility, its ecosystems are constantly stressed, both from natural forces such as fire and drought, and from conditions introduced by one of its most recent and most aggressive colonizing species: Homo sapiens.

FINGERPRINTS OF A DEPARTED SEA

The creation of this remarkable environment began in Cretaceous times, 65 million years back, when most of the Southwest was under water. This was a shallow ocean, periodically expanding and shrinking, and at what we now call Mesa Verde it deposited a 2,000-foot layer of silt, including a mud clay now called Mancos shale. This dark gray shale, the mesa's oldest rock, is exposed along the park entrance road where it climbs the hill to Morefield Campground.

After the shale came progressive waves of other deposits—Point Lookout sandstone, the Menefee formation, and finally Cliff House sandstone. Because this mineral-depositing sea kept rising and receding, layers of these different sedimentary rocks are woven into the mesa with a complexity that can confuse even geologists. But visitors can easily find fingerprints of the departed sea: ripple marks from Cretaceous waves, frozen in the alcoves that shelter Long House and Balcony House.

From the cliff-like north rim at a peak elevation of 8,571 feet, the cuesta slopes gently toward the south, dropping 2,500 feet until it collapses into the trench that cradles the Mancos River. Like many other southwestern mesas and dramatic sandstone spire formations such as Monument Valley, it's the eroded remnant of a pediment, a sloping mountain base that once connected Mesa Verde with the La Plata and San Juan Mountains. A few million years of moving water patiently chewed them apart.

Over those same years, water trickling down Mesa Verde collected into intermittent streams and scratched fifteen almost parallel, steep-walled canyons into the cuesta, north to south, like a cat raking wood with its claws. The canyons dissect the south mesa into a puzzle of outstretched fingers. Nordenskiöld admired the view of this "intricate labyrinth" even as he complained of the "very great difficulties" of riding across the mesa.

The varied consistency of those Cretaceous sea deposits was responsible for the alcoves that the Ancestral Puebloans eventually would adopt for their shelters. Cliff House sandstone, the topmost formation of the mesa, is porous, so water seeps through until it encounters denser shale. Then the water percolates along the dividing line between the two rock formations until it seeps out the canyon wall. Whenever it freezes inside the rock, it expands and pops off a piece of sandstone. Most sandstone canyons on the Colorado Plateau are pocked with alcoves, but Mesa Verde has been endowed with an extraordinary number—probably due to the high elevation and frequent freeze-thaw cycles.

Lichen-covered Cretaceous sandstone.

OPPOSITE: *Point Lookout at the entrance to Mesa Verde National Park.*

In winter the Mesa Verde can have an accumulation of as much as three feet of snow.

A CHALLENGING CLIMATE

A shawl of snow cloaks the canyon rims and depths of Mesa Verde with a romantic, thoroughly engaging beauty. The softness and silence are wonderful to experience—for modern visitors equipped with layers of fleece, waterproof boots and the prospect of returning to a heated car.

For the people living here 800 and more years back, the climate presented serious challenges. A heavy snowfall probably generated little cheer among the Ancestral Puebloans, especially if the clouds persisted for days, choking off all prospects for passive solar heating. Some archeologists wonder whether the Ancestral Puebloans might have vacated the cliff dwellings in deepest winter, finding or making temporary shelter at lower elevations. (The mesa's deer population migrates downslope, and it would have made sense to follow the game animals if they were plentiful). But this is only a theory, and it has its problems. Cold air spilling off the slopes often makes the basin around the mesa even colder. And would people have left their vital food caches unguarded?

In modern times, January highs at park headquarters average 40° F (4° C) and lows average 18° F (-8° C). The coldest temperature yet recorded on the mesa is -20° F (-29° C). Summers are usually moderate, with an average July high of 87° F (31° C) and low of 57° F (14° C). Precipitation is stingy enough to classify the mesa as semi-arid, with a modern average of 18 inches (46 cm) a year. However, a 3-foot (91 cm) accumulation of snow is not unusual. Tree-ring studies suggest that the climate in Ancestral Puebloan times was not much different from today, except perhaps during the most stubborn droughts.

Mesa Verde also presented its residents with another challenge: no permanent stream other than the Mancos River, whose deep canyon forms the eastern boundary of the park. Surveys have found more than 200 springs, seeps and sandstone basins on the mesa that retain rainwater for a few days, but many of these sources dry up during long stretches without precipitation. The Ancestral Puebloans would have had to practice the most rigorous water conservation imaginable.

To thrive in Mesa Verde's climate, its residents would have had to learn to read its widely varied environments, making judgments about temperature, rainfall patterns and soil fertility with a skill that modern city dwellers can hardly imagine. In their own way, the Ancestral Puebloans would have had to be scientists, hard workers, survivors —and lucky.

LIFE ON THE MESA

Thanks to floral and faunal remains uncovered during excavations in the park, we know a great deal about the biology of Mesa Verde during Ancestral Puebloan times. It generally resembles what park visitors find today, with some important exceptions. During our relatively short window of occupation on the mesa, humans have wrought serious changes.

The pollen record of Ancestral Pueblo times tells us that the people stripped the mesa of much of its forest for firewood and building materials, and these woodlands rebounded very slowly after their departure in the late 1200s. A pinyon-juniper forest takes 200 to 300 years to regenerate, a tall conifer forest even longer.

Modern civilization has altered Mesa Verde's biology at least as profoundly. Early park management in the 20th century waged war on predators and what were then considered varmints, including coyotes, prairie dogs, and even porcupines. A 1932 ranger's report targeted the tree-gnawing porcupine in particularly colorful language: "Since I can mention nothing in favor of the porcupine, this report deals entirely with his evils. I have tried to present the evidence with which I accuse the rodent and which I hope will convict him, so that his numbers can be materially reduced ..." Hunting outside the park boundaries also has changed the balance of nature throughout the entire region. The Mexican gray wolf vanished from Colorado in 1944; the state's last grizzly was killed in 1976. Gone from Mesa Verde are the river otter and black-footed ferret. Bighorn sheep were eliminated, then reintroduced, and are still extremely scarce in the park. The river's native fish are now endangered by several predatory introduced species, upstream

Mesa Verde provides habitat for 200 species of birds, 74 mammals, 16 reptiles and five amphibians.

CLOCKWISE FROM TOP: *Red-tailed hawk, coyote, porcupine, badger, mule deer, collared lizard.*

Pinyon and juniper forests, thriving on modest rainfall, cloak the surface of Mesa Verde, whereas the moist microclimates of the canyons sustain dense shrubs and occasionally Douglas-fir.

dams and contamination from mine, farm and urban wastes.

The Rocky Mountain mule deer is the most abundant large animal roaming the park in recent years, although the deer population is frequently in flux. In the late 1960s, park managers became concerned that the large number of deer summering on the mesa—a study estimated 4,500 to 5,200—was overgrazing the range. The park undertook a controversial effort to trim the herd, and by 1976 only one-fourth that number of deer remained. But as grazing improved, the herd continued to decline—the result, researchers finally realized, of the increased population of predatory coyotes, bobcats and mountain lions that had arisen to take advantage of the abundance of fawns. Eventually the deer rebounded, and the park's wildlife managers took the lesson to heart. The fortunes of any one species provoke ripples up and down the food chain to the benefit or detriment of others, but in the long run, nature is a self-correcting loop. She does not, however, like to be rushed.

Wildlife on the mesa also thrives and struggles with the whims of the seasons. A wet year will produce more plant seeds and pinyon nuts, which a population boom in rodents arises to exploit. Then follows an improvement in the lot of their predators, such as snakes, weasels, bobcats and raptors. Despite the pressures on their habitats, an amazing variety of small mammals and birds inhabit the park. There are more than a dozen species of bats, six species of squirrels, gray and red foxes, spotted and striped skunks. The Steller's jay commands attention with its raucous call, but the large, silently soaring birds are equally captivating: eight species of hawks, bald and golden eagles, the turkey vulture and the common raven.

Unlike some taller mountains in the Southwest, Mesa Verde doesn't function as a biological "sky island," isolated from its neighbors. Most animal species migrate onto and off the mesa, depending on season and food supplies—which is why some have vanished from the mesa even though hunting and trapping are forbidden in national parks. There are a handful of unique species that have passed their evolutionary lives on the mesa, however—most notably the Mesa Verde tiger beetle, so named for its distinctive orange and black shell.

Within the national park's eighty-one square miles are several distinct botanical communities. The mountain shrub community, featuring gambel oak, Utah serviceberry, and mountain mahogany, is the largest, covering the higher slopes to the north. The "pygmy forest" of pinyon pine and Utah juniper is the next largest. Although the pinyon and juniper lack the majestic stature of the big conifers, their gnarly textures have a beauty all their own— look closely; there's *geography* in their bark—and they are phenomenally useful trees. Old-growth pinyon and juniper are cratered with cavities that provide nests and food caches for birds and rodents. Ancestral Puebloans used juniper berries as medicine and food flavoring. A historic Pueblo practice was to mix them with chopped meat, stuff it into a deer stomach, and roast the package. Pinyon nuts pack a punch of tasty fat and protein. Biologists think the pinyon-juniper forest, which thrives on modest rainfall, ought to get more respect. As Mesa Verde Natural Resource Manager George San Miguel says, wryly but seriously, "Like the indigenous peoples that lived here before us, perhaps the thrifty P-J would make a good role model for modern peoples of the Southwest."

The towering Douglas-fir forest crowns the mesa's highlands, but its range is relatively small—less than seven square miles. A nine-acre colony of quaking aspen erupts in an annual fall festival of brilliant gold. The riparian cottonwood, gambel oak, and a relic stand of bigtooth maple also contribute their color.

The canyons provide a great variety of plant habitats because of their wide variations in elevation and microclimates. Pinyon and juniper make tentative excursions down the slopes, then yield to shrubs such as mountain mahogany, serviceberry, and skunkbush sumac that thrive on shallow soil. The canyon floors are high desert ecosystems, medleys of sagebrush, grasses, and cacti.

A few plant species are unique to Mesa Verde, occurring nowhere else on earth: Mesa Verde stickseed, Mesa Verde wandering aletes, Schmoll's milkvetch, and Cliff Palace milkvetch. The latter, an easily overlooked legume that grows in clumps just two inches high, is in serious trouble, as it occurs only on rimrock that happens to provide good views of cliff dwellings in the canyons below. Despite the park's efforts, off-trail foot traffic has trampled two clusters near Cliff Palace and Sun Temple down to half their former population.

Weeds are another growing concern in the park—a "weed" in this context being any species that isn't a native. Biologists have identified eighty-one non-natives, and the number keeps growing. Some arrived with farming operations decades ago; others were introduced in what park biologists now call misguided efforts to revegetate park land after fire or construction. Modern park policy is to preserve the integrity of the natural environment, and non-natives disrupt it by crowding out natives and changing animal feeding patterns. The most noxious weeds now worrying Mesa Verde include Canada thistle, musk thistle, cheatgrass, and tamarisk. Spraying, uprooting and even biological controls—releasing insects hostile to target plants—have all been tried on a limited basis, but without significant success to date.

Left to her own devices, nature will, over time, perfectly manage the intricate gearworks of every biological community. When the tribe of humanity tinkers and meddles, trying to manage it to suit our needs, there erupts a chain of unintended consequences.

Wildfire is not new to Mesa Verde; however, in the nine dry years from 1996 through 2004, five enormous summer fires scorched 36 square miles within the park.

THE ECOLOGY OF FIRE AND DROUGHT

As alarming and devastating as they seem to us, forest and grassland fires are part of the natural rhythm of the land, and Mesa Verde is no exception. On the average, lightning triggers some sixty

Crucial wildlife habitat was lost in each successive Mesa Verde wildfire.

fires a year within the park, most of them inconsequential. But a long, stubborn drought that unfolded in the mid-1990s combined forces with these natural triggers and a century of unnatural fuel buildup to provoke a string of fires unprecedented in recorded history.

The practice of allowing cattle to graze on park land had ended in the 1920s, but the park service continued a policy of 100 percent fire suppression. When the 1980s and early '90s brought an unusually rainy cycle, an already vigorous undergrowth rejoiced and grew luxurious. The consequences were disastrous. In the nine dry years from 1996 through 2004, Mesa Verde suffered five enormous summer fires that all together scorched 36 square miles within the national park boundary—45 percent of the park's total land area.

In August 1996, the Chapin 5 fire burned 4,781 acres in the park and cost $2 million to fight. The battle engaged 5 helicopters, 6 air tankers, 16 engines and 649 firefighters.

In the parched summer of 2000, uncontrollable blazes twice attacked the mesa. The Bircher Fire started July 20 with a lightning strike on the Bircher farm near the park entrance. For the next nine days it raged through the pinyon-juniper forest, mostly inside the park boundary. The fire burned 45 percent of the entire national park, the most destructive blaze in park history. At times the flames reached 300 feet, too fierce for fire retardant to work or for crews to approach them. The park closed for two weeks. Then on August 2, lightning ignited another fire on the Ute Mountain Ute Reservation just west of Mesa Verde, and two days later it too broke out of control. Mesa Verde evacuated visitors again, just twelve hours after the park had reopened following the Bircher Fire. The new Pony Fire burned nine days, torched six square miles of reservation land and two more square miles of the national park, destroying a ranger station, bookstore, ranger contact station and shelters on Wetherill Mesa.

In July 2002, the Long Mesa Fire destroyed three historic park structures, including two employee houses, a million-gallon water tank, and a sewer treatment building. Again the park closed for ten days. And in July 2003 a dry thunderstorm ignited 400 acres in the Balcony House Complex fires in the national park, and hundreds more on the reservation.

There were nuggets of good news in all this. No human lives were lost, none of the cliff dwellings was seriously damaged, and the fires have even revealed previously unrecorded archeological sites. The 1996 Chapin 5 fire uncovered 372 sites such as check dams and depressions where walls had once stood.

But the devastation was profound, especially in wildlife habitat. Grasses, shrubs and gambel oak stands return quickly, but an old-growth pinyon-juniper forest may take 200 to 300 years to regenerate. Park biologists are not sure the burned stands of ponderosa will ever return; they were small communities, and new seedlings face tough battles with fast-growing shrubs. Immigrant Canada thistle and musk thistle race to colonize burn zones, competing with many native plants.

Massive erosion follows big fires such as these. The flames can literally bake soil on canyon slopes, killing bacteria and sterilizing the soil so that nothing will grow in it. The ground becomes hydrophobic; water flows over it as if on bathroom tile and scours the canyon floors. In the two years after the Bircher and Pony fires, rangers measured unusual flash floods running nine to thirteen feet deep in some canyons—and these happened in dry years. Archeological sites have been threatened by the erosion, and intense heat actually destroyed some petroglyphs at Battleship Rock.

The drought has also encouraged some unwelcome wildlife: the pinyon engraver beetle, a rice grain-sized pest that attacks drought-stressed pinyon trees. A 2003 Mesa Verde park biologist's report renders the forest's outlook in stark words: "The situation has deteriorated into a negative feedback loop where continuing drought touches off catastrophic wildfires, which encourages bark beetles to wipe out forests, which fuels more fires … The three-pronged assault on Mesa Verde's evergreen forests from drought, fire and pathogens will not stop until the climate shifts back closer to historical norms."

Some biologists believe that even these "catastrophic" fires—to use the human-centric word for them—are a normal burn cycle, nature's form of all-out housecleaning and rebuilding. Small, lightning-sparked fires of less than an acre and patches of trees killed by fungus or insects are also ecologically valuable, because they create open spaces in the forest and provide diverse habitats that support more species. The park's dilemma in trying to manage these fires is to somehow balance nature's order (still imperfectly understood) with the need to protect life, property, and the irreplaceable relics of human cultures.

There is healthy debate over how much we humans have exacerbated the forests' problems, from the last century's forest management practices to the likely provocation of global climate change. We know from tree-ring records that drought is a regular visitor to the arid Southwest, and that the Ancestral Puebloans learned to cope with it without the benefits of electric-powered wells and firefighting aircraft. But we also know that their population throughout the Southwest was far smaller than ours, and that they did not consider their pueblos as resources to be preserved at all costs: they moved whenever environmental conditions seemed to demand it. And they used fire to clear their fields for farming.

A living park? Decidedly. More than seven centuries ago the people of Mesa Verde faced an environmental crisis and apparent social challenges; today another culture is confronted with different but equally perplexing difficulties. The lovely but prickly southwestern landscape has always tested the people who stake their claims on it. Nature will make no exception for us.

Mesa Verde, the living park.

EXPLORING FURTHER

A pottery shard out of its context is meaningless. Left where it was dropped 800 years ago, it can help archeologists fill in the story of the ancient Southwest. The exact location of any relic can tell its age, its use, or possibly reveal a migration pattern.

The Archaeological Resources Protection Act of 1979 outlawed pothunting and scrounging for arrowheads on U.S. government property. All southwestern states now have similar laws on state lands. Beyond laws, everyday ethics tell us to respect whatever artifacts we may find.

It's thrilling to find an unmapped, unprotected remnant of ancient Pueblo civilizations in the Southwest, but it's vital to respect it. Don't climb on walls or enter rooms. Never touch petroglyphs; body oil deteriorates them.

Some prehistoric artifacts on the market are authentic and legally taken from private land. But the market teems with pots harvested illegally, and the government can seize them without compensating the new owner. Reputable dealers say there are a "terrific number" of fakes out there, made by "artists" so proficient that even experts sometimes are unable to tell the difference.

Many southwestern artists legitimately replicate Ancestral Puebloan ceramics using 12th-century techniques and sign with their own 21st-century names. Collecting these will cost at most a tenth of the (maybe) real thing.

VISITING SITES

Visit pueblo sites near sunrise or sunset. The crowds are absent, and the soft light and deep shadows accent the architectural drama. Take advantage of guided tours and talks. Park rangers know far more than the brochures tell.

Explore the ecology of a site. Scope out its relationship to water sources and where crops might have been cultivated. Plot the arc of the sun across the winter sky. Carry binoculars and a compass. Watch for unadvertised petroglyphs, small game, and snakes.

Within 150 miles of Mesa Verde lies a fascinating education in ancient America, including:

Colorado: Ute Mountain Ute Tribal Park, Anasazi Heritage Center, and Canyons of the Ancients which has the highest density of archeological sites in the U.S.

New Mexico: Chaco Culture National Historical Park; and Aztec Ruins, El Morro, Bandelier, and Petroglyph national monuments.

Utah: Hovenweep National Monument.

Arizona: Canyon de Chelly, Navajo, Wupatki, Montezuma Castle, and Walnut Canyon national monuments; Petrified Forest and Grand Canyon national parks; and Homolovi Ruins State Park.

In Mexico, the lonely but spectacular remnants of Paquimé, southwest of El Paso are vital to understanding the Ancestral Pueblo world.

MORE READING

Endlessly absorbing, and full of twists, turns, and controversies, the literary journey into the Native American cultures of North America includes:

Anasazi America. David E. Stuart, University of New Mexico Press 2000.
Ancient North America: The Archaeology of a Continent. Brian M. Fagan, Thames and Hudson 1995.
Archaeology of the Southwest. Linda S. Cordell, Academic Press 1997.
The People: Indians of the American Southwest. Steven Trimble, School of American Research 1993.
Prehistoric Warfare in the American Southwest. Steven A. LeBlanc, The University of Utah Press 1999.
Richard Wetherill: Anasazi. Frank McNitt, University of New Mexico Press 1966.
Those Who Came Before: Archaeology in the National Park System. Robert and Florence Lister, Western National Parks Association 2000.

ABOUT THE AUTHOR

Lawrence W. Cheek is a native southwesterner whose passions include archeology, architecture, natural history and the environment. He worked as a reporter, critic, and editor for the *Tucson Citizen* and later edited *City Magazine* in Tucson. His thirteen other books about the Southwest include ones on the Navajo Long Walk and Frank Lloyd Wright's Arizona work. He is now the architecture critic for the *Seattle Post-Intelligencer*.

ABOUT THE PHOTOGRAPHER

George Huey is a landscape, travel, and natural history photographer who has been called a "poet of the Southwest" by the National Geographic Society. His work has appeared in dozens of magazines here and abroad such as *Architectural Digest, Arizona Highways, Audubon, Conde Nast Traveler, Islands, Elle, French Geo, German Geo, Men's Journal, National Geographic Traveler, Newsweek, Outside,* and *Travel & Leisure*. He has photographed several books about the Southwest, including *The Southwest: Gold, God & Grandeur,* and *Guide To America's Outdoors: Southern Rockies*.